Homework Heroes

Drew and Cynthia Johnson

with Introduction by

Priscilla L. Vail, M. A. T.

KAPLAN BOOKS

New York   London   Toronto   Sydney   Singapore

Kaplan Publishing
Published by Simon & Schuster, Inc.
1230 Avenue of the Americas
New York, NY 10020

For bulk sales to schools, colleges, and universities, please contact:
Order Department, Simon & Schuster, Inc., 100 Front Street,
Riverside, NJ 08075. Phone: (800) 223-2336. Fax: (800) 943-9831.

For information regarding special discounts for other bulk purchases,
please contact Simon & Schuster Special Sales at 1-800-456-6798 or
business@simonandschuster.com

Editor: Beth Grupper
Cover Design: Cheung Tai
Interior Design: Richard Oriolo
Interior Layout and Production: Anaxos, Inc.

Manufactured in the United States of America

January 2002
10 9 8 7 6 5 4 3 2 1

Library of Congress Cataloging-in-Publication Data

ISBN: 0-7432-2258-X

Table of Contents

Chapter 2: A Review of Basic Math Concepts

for Grades 3-5

Chapter 3: A Review of Basic English

 Concepts for Grades 3-5

Chapter 6: Fencing Lessons

Homework Heroes: Grades 3-5

HOMEWORK IS A FACT OF life for most children, but parents are often confused about their role in this daily drama and concerned about meshing homework with the general dynamics of personal and family life. While homework sometimes causes frustration and arguments for you and your child, it can also be a vehicle for cooperation, a source of pride and accomplishment, and an opportunity for fun and creativity.

Fantasy? No.

From my own experiences as a full-time teacher for over a quarter of a century, a parent of four children, a grandmother of six, a student of learning, a curriculum planner, and a designer and leader of teacher and parenting workshops across this country and abroad, I have some:

complexities to explore and strategies to share

cautions to mention and techniques to offer

issues to highlight and research to quarry

questions to raise and purposes to reinforce

These combinations can help you and your child reduce negatives to a minimum and enhance the positive aspects of a daily reality. You can be Homework Heroes to one another, and this book is designed to set you on your way.

If you have read some of my books or articles, or have heard me speak, some of what follows here may sound familiar. Good, that means we are already friends. For new acquaintances, my message is both realistic and optimistic:

Your child can succeed.

You can survive.

There is life after homework.

Collectors, Givers, and Tool Users

Students in grades three to five are collectors, givers, and tool users. They absorb and use language (speaking, listening, reading, and writing), humor (puns and double entendre), numeracy (cardinal and ordinal numbers and process signs), large and small motor systems, intuition, and empathy. Children this age are solemnly interested in rules and codes, although they don't always abide by them. Restraint is unknown to them, and by the end of the day they are usually exhausted. Therefore, well-designed homework in grades three to five should emphasize review and rumination, offering opportunities for projects that match the student's internal rhythm, stamina, and intellectual level. These are years to solidify reading skills and to nourish and expand comprehension and language in math as well as language arts.

Because students in these years are gatherers instead of winnowers, such exercises as "finding the main idea" may overwhelm them. Every idea is a main idea to a gatherer. And finally, because of their natures, they prefer vigor to rigor.

As a parent, you will want to provide structures and examples of orderliness that show children how to organize themselves. Read on for some specific suggestions and tips on how to do this.

Here are twenty questions you need to address as you think about homework. This structure will provide a banister to support and guide us as we walk our way up through this sometimes conflict-ridden topic.

1. What is the homework policy at your child's school?

2. What is each individual teacher's homework policy?

3. What is your homework policy as a parent?

4. Who has ownership of homework?

5. How does homework solidify or undermine eight relationships?

6. Time: Does your child use it well?

7. Space: Where is homework to be done?

8. Do you have a Time and Space Homework Pact?

9. How long should homework take?

10. What about boredom and drudgery?

11. Does your child have the prerequisite reading skills to manage assigned homework?

12. Do your child's developmental and language levels match the assigned tasks?

13. Do your child's handwriting skills match the assigned tasks?

14. Do your child's study skills and learning styles match the assigned tasks?

15. What if your child has dyslexia or a learning disability?

16. Are your child's emotional habits and considerations taken into account?

17. Do your child's memory skills match the expectations of the homework?

18. Does the homework attach new concepts to ones that are already familiar?

19. Does your child's homework promote privacy, participation, and enjoying your kid?

20. Do you watch the "Plimsoll Line"? (No, it's not a new television show. Puzzled? Read on!)

Let's look at these twenty questions, one by one, and explore their implications for children in grades three to five.

1. What is the homework policy at your child's school?

If homework is going to demand the amount of time schools expect and require, the school philosophy should be clear and articulated. Is homework for:

reinforcement of concepts?

extension of concepts?

preparation for concepts?

development of independent learning?

enjoyment and expansion of creativity?

drill and practice, including test preparation?

time filling?

You have every right to ask for, encourage, or even demand a statement from the school on its homework philosophy. If such a statement is not in place, or in writing, it is reasonable to ask the administration when they would be able to have one ready: next week, next month, three months? What would they like you, and other parents, to do in the meantime? Parents (and students) deserve this information.

Since many schools have not articulated a homework policy, it may take a little time and cajoling, but never underestimate the power a coordinated group wields. Be polite but firm, remembering that schools, like most institutions, move at a glacial pace.

2. What is each individual teacher's homework policy? Are each teacher's ideas consistent with what the school has stated, and among each other?

Usually, homeroom teachers will outline the homework policy on back-to-school night or in a newsletter sent home early in the year. If they don't, most teachers will be glad to answer individual parent questions on the topic. If a teacher has not thought through this issue, he or she needs to do so.

Through fourth grade, students generally work in a homeroom with one head teacher who makes the major decisions. Then, starting in fifth grade, their education becomes departmentalized; they have different teachers for different subjects. If teachers from different disciplines compare notes about homework assignments and plan together, well and good. If they don't, the students can get caught in an overlap overload of assignments. A well-considered school policy may save lives!

If your child is caught in a homework crunch, first talk to the teacher(s) involved. If that doesn't work, make an appointment with the administrator. Base your comments on what the school has stated as homework policy. This will be much more effective than what might be interpreted as "whining about Johnny."

3. What is your homework policy as a parent?

Many children at this level have active after-school lives. At the same time, the volume of homework increases and long-term projects enter the scene. One mother said to me, "Job? I've got three kids. I've got homework! How could I have a job?"

As a parent, you need to articulate a family homework policy just as you expect schools and teachers to outline their policies.

For example, one family I know says, "During the week, we all have our routines for homework, bedtime, and adult responsibilities. When the weekend comes, we need to have time for fun together, but we still have chores and homework. For us, Saturday is the time to do them. Adults do the errands and transport kids to athletic games or practices. Our kids do their homework, even if it means they have to get up early. By the end of the day, the chores are done, the homework is finished, and we can go out for supper, hit the movies, rent a video, or have friends over. It's important to give fun an important place on the schedule."

4. Who has ownership of homework?

Let there be no fuzziness here: your child owns and is responsible for the assignments; your child is the one to do the work. Let your child own the triumphs. Anything else is theft.

Does this mean no help? Of course not. You should help by providing the time and space in which to work on assignments, offering encouragement, listening to spelling words, admiring a product, praising diligence, helping to sound out an unfamiliar word, or running through flashcards. You should be interested and supportive, but your child owns the homework.

What if your administrative assistant reformats and collates your child's research paper on the explorers? Or what if a classmate has this kind of external support and your child doesn't? A fair solution is to clip a little note to the cover of the report saying, "Our whole family was interested in this project and we were glad to lend a hand." This removes any question of cheating. In one school where parents were worried that this issue was skewing the grades (and it was), the teacher set out two tables, saying, "If you were lucky enough to have help at home on your project, please put it here. If you are the sole creator of your project, please put it on this table." This made the distinctions very clear, and each type had its own legitimate glory.

5. How does homework solidify or undermine eight relationships?

parent/child	child/parent
parent/teacher	child/teacher
parent/family	child/family
parent/self	child/self

Understanding how these relationships interconnect, and being sure all are in good repair, separately and jointly, is fundamental to effective vigilance, your privilege as a parent.

In the **parent/child** homework relationship, you have ten responsibilities: structure the procedures, guarantee a suitable setting for the work, help when invited, be available for consultation without doing the child's work, admire the effort and the product, provide a homework checklist, help your child establish productive work habits, model the behavior you expect from your kid, establish the Time and Space Homework Pact (see question 8), and abide by it.

Because of the particular demands at this age, you may be called on to take your child to the library over the weekend or make a quick shopping trip for vital material.

In the **child/parent** homework relationship, your child should be working to establish feelings of responsibility, diligence without dependency, and pride in accomplishment. Children this age need assurance that they are capable of doing the job independently, but that they have not been cast loose.

In the **parent/teacher** homework relationship, you should ask teachers these questions:

What are your goals for this year?

How can we help achieve them?

How do you want us to contact you if necessary?

How do you want us to deal with overload or with errors we see our child making?

You need to be friendly and supportive, yet honest when there is a problem. If your child's homework is stressful, or takes too long, state it in a "we" message. "We had trouble last night getting the work done. How should we all proceed?"

When talking with a teacher, establish yourself as an ally, not an adversary. Thus, start by mentioning something positive about the class: "Danny so enjoyed hearing you read *The Jungle Books,* and now sprinkles 'Oh best beloved' into his family conversations." Then, being descriptive instead of critical, you should explain the situation and ask for a team approach in solving it.

Here's an insider's tip: *never* pounce on a teacher in the hall or at the door of the classroom as the day is starting. The teacher's proper focus is on the group: orchestrating the day, drawing the group into

When your child is stumped, you may have to supply some coaching. Be glad your child feels comfortable asking. For example, one mother whose child was struggling to write a biographical paper (without having been taught how) said, "Tell me about this person, just as though we were riding along in the car and you were telling me about someone interesting you had just met." The child talked, the mother listened and asked a few questions, then together they discussed which were the most interesting and important details about the person's life, and the child said, "Oh, I get it." This took time but the results were impressive, and the child received a successful strategy . . . more valuable by far than an answer.

the lesson, generating excitement, soothing feelings, and infusing courage. Diverting the teacher's concentration at such a time is like delivering a telephone message to a conductor about to raise the baton. Instead, send a note saying what you want to talk about, how much time you think you need, and suggest a time, or ask the teacher to set an alternative.

Here's another insider's teacher tip: stay in touch with the teacher all year long. Most people connect in the beginning and end of the year, few connect in the middle. By doing this, you will have more undivided attention and can use this time to express appreciation for what is going well. You will earn big brownie points!

In the **child/teacher** homework relationship, your child needs to be totally honest with the teacher: "I loved that project," or "My hand gets too tired to write that much," or "I don't like to read." When your child is honest, the teacher can do what teachers go into teaching to do: help. Your child also needs to ask for clear assignments, written not spoken, with time to copy them down. He also needs to know where to put completed work.

In the **parent/family** homework relationship, you are the coordinator and producer of the show, integrating each child's needs, and coordinating demands for attention with the competing needs of siblings, spouse, the dog, or a grandparent. (Being a grandparent myself allows me to use that sequence.) Thus, plan some quiet time where family members have free choice as long as it's relatively quiet. All family members need collective peace as well as collective urgency. You can establish this priority.

In the **child/family** homework relationship, insofar as possible, your child should do homework with its attendant demands for help, quiet, and so forth, when others in the family are similarly engaged. This means that each child in the family should have an ample supply of enjoyable projects to do solo while others are working. Children may also need to share available work spaces.

In the **parent/self** homework relationship, you should get a life! Be gentle with yourself. You are a person, not road kill. Yoga, music, athletics, computers, and opportunities for adult companionship are nourishing to the spirit, and, by the way, good for physical health.

In the **child/self** homework relationship, you want your child to behave responsibly, feel proud, be honest about what is hard and what is easy, enjoy successes, and save time and emotional energy for developing personal passions.

6. Time: Does your child use it well?

First, be sure your child really knows how to tell time. Lots of kids in grades three to five appear to know how because they call off the numbers on their digital watches. This surface skill may mask an underlying confusion. Be sure your child can use an analog watch and clock. Why? A digital timepiece shows only the present moment, giving no indication of what came before or what is around the corner. Planning requires a sense of past, present, and future. If your child can actively plan her homework, she can feel in charge. If your child doesn't have the tools for planning, she is a constant victim; homework is something that happens to her instead of something she makes happen. A solid concept of time, including a sense of the passing of time (technically called *elapsing time*), has a big and benevolent effect on your child's academic future. It is important to consolidate this skill now.

You can promote this by trying to speak in concise time language: "It's five-fifteen now. You need to start your homework in fifteen minutes," or "We have ten minutes until supper. Do you want to throw the ball around?"

This is the age to focus on the concept of elapsing time, meaning how long something takes to do, and how it fits into the time allowance provided for the task. There are literally *millions* of adults who have destroyed potentially satisfying personal and business relationships because they never developed the concept of elapsing time. If you don't understand the concept, you can't monitor it. If you can't monitor it, it is not part of your planning apparatus. You lose, big time.

Here is a simple, free, effective strategy for teaching elapsing time:

Say to your child, "Look at the clock when you start to do your homework. When you think ten minutes have gone by, look up at the clock. Are you early, late, or on the money? Do this for five days. You will begin to see your own pattern. If you are usually early, try to stretch out your sense of ten minutes. If you are usually late, try to rein it in. If you are usually on the money, can you predict thirty minutes?"

Have your child progress from ten minutes to thirty and then to an hour. Try three hours. A child who can do this develops an internal alarm clock that will be helpful in getting places on time and also fitting work into time slots allotted for it. When a teacher says, "Write for the next thirty minutes on a memorable experience," your child will be able to pace herself and finish in the allotted time.

This works in real life as well as in homework. If you are due to leave in an hour, do you have a sense of how much time is left before you need to get dressed? Grownups can practice this skill, too.

Once the concept of elapsing time is established, you can help your child with what is technically called *projected time*. For example, you, as an adult, need to be able to predict how long it will take to fold the laundry, make the salad, balance the checkbook, and jog two miles. Similarly, your child needs to estimate how long it will take to learn her spelling words, make the mask for the play, put her equipment in her soccer bag, and practice the trombone.

A truth: predicting required time depends on recognizing the passing of time.

7. Space: Where is homework to be done?

It is important for you to identify, guarantee, and equip a place for your child to work, encouraging your child to give it a name: Homework Heaven, the Studying Spot, or the Serious Desk. Your child should establish the habit of going there to do homework, leaving when the job is done. It should *not* be in front of the television!

It is important for you and your child to acknowledge that surroundings influence concentration and focus . . . as well as their opposites. Some places are designed for fun and relaxation. Your child needs to choose the setting according to the purpose. The following section offers some suggestions for choosing a homework location.

8. Do you have a Time and Space Homework Pact?

You and your child should settle on a Time and Space Homework Pact, a family policy of when and where homework is to be done. To craft such a pact, you and your child need to agree on these two aspects of homework planning while taking into account student preferences and family realities.

First, let's think about the time aspect of the pact. Your child may want to sit right down after school and polish off the homework. Or she may need to have something to eat, play with the guinea pig, skip rope, or log on to the computer for a while before revisiting academics. If your child has an after-school activity on Tuesdays and Thursdays, she may need to have supper first on those evenings and then tackle the homework. She also needs to decide whether to try to do all the homework at one sitting or break it into chunks. If you agree on the latter, does she want to do the hard subjects first, saving the easier ones for later, or vice versa? If the pact is going to work, it must reflect and include your child's individual needs and preferences.

Regarding space, your child may like to do homework in the bedroom. But if she is like many others, the bedroom has connotations of drifting and dreaming. That atmosphere may override the purposefulness studying requires. If so, she may do better studying in the living room, the den, or at the kitchen table. No single answer is right for all children. Take your home environment and your child's preferences into account.

When all the issues have been fleshed out, you and your child need to agree on the rules, and then write and sign a pact that will remain in effect for six weeks. During those six weeks there will be no further discussion of whens and wheres. After that, all issues can be renegotiated. This fair and comprehensive approach eliminates nightly bargaining, which is a great relief to all concerned.

Major tools for the Time and Space Pact are the three C's: clock, calendar, and color-coding. (See question 6 for additional comments about time and digital and analog clocks). These three Cs make time a visible tool for the child who didn't catch on spontaneously, for whom clocks and calendars have simply been adult-devised impositions. Furthermore, when assignments are laid out in space as well as in time—on a calendar for instance—it is easier for a child this age to resist procrastination. If your child sees that today is Tuesday and the weekly spelling test is on Wednesday, she can *see* as well as *be told* that it's time to learn those words.

Be sure your child is comfortable with this helpful tool. Get a big calendar that shows at least a month at a time. At the end of each day, ask your child to draw a little rebus of something that happened: it rained, Sam threw up, Sally had a birthday, we had a school play, Granny came to visit. Look ahead to important events such as holidays and birthdays. Once the calendar has a week or two of notations, your child can go back over the timeline asking such questions as, "How many days ago was that big rainstorm?" "How many people in our family have birthdays this month?" "Which day of the week is usually your favorite?" You and your child, together, also need to color-code the calendar, marking in whatever colors you have chosen to represent regular events such as music lessons or athletic practices. Anchoring personal, physical experiences to the abstraction of a chart of white boxes brings the concept of time to life. Your child will come to understand the calendar, and people use tools they understand.

It goes without saying that you, as parents, must model the behaviors you expect from your child. It's not fair to say, "Oops. I forgot! We have to go out in the car. How about doing your homework on the back seat, and I'll buy you a bag of chips and a soda to make it more pleasant?"

You and your child can also share your pact with the teachers who, one hopes, will bless and cooperate with the endeavor. Situations in which parents, children, and teachers work together are ideal.

A sample pact for this age might say:

On weeknights, homework time will begin right after supper. Thus, athletics and academics will not interfere with one another. Homework time will be uninterrupted for the allocated amount of time. Work will be done at the dining-room table and the atmosphere will be quiet.

On weekends, homework assignments are to be completed on Saturday, so the evening will be free for fun.

This pact will remain in effect until _____(date).

Signed: _____
(your child)

_____
(you)

Date:_____

Post the pact on the refrigerator door, the family bulletin board, or some other serious, public place.

9. How long should homework take?

A rule of thumb in many thoughtful schools is ten minutes per night per grade level: thirty minutes for third-graders, forty minutes for fourth-graders, fifty minutes for fifth-graders. Even if your child's school has adopted a rule of thumb, everyone needs to remember that children this age work at different paces, so a rule of thumb is not a law.

If homework is expected to take thirty, forty, or fifty minutes but your child is spending fifty, sixty, or seventy minutes (or variations thereof), is it because teacher time estimates are short? With students this age, it is important to assess whether assignments take too long because of known or undetected difficulties with reading, unreliable reading comprehension skills, or interrupted concentration or daydreaming, issues we will address in more detail in subsequent sections.

If homework is too hard or takes too long, you, or you and your child together, should be open with the teacher as suggested in question 5. In preparation for such conversations, you and your child should keep a nightly log of genuine TOT (Time on Task) versus "book holding."

10. What about boredom and drudgery?

Sometimes, to save face, children say, "I'm bored" or "This is boring," when they really mean, "I'm scared I can't do this," or "This is too hard." In such cases, the trick is to get right at the problem, break down the task, and help with whatever components are getting in the way. The longer the masquerade continues, the harder it is to get the real, necessary job done.

Real boredom exists when teachers assign worksheets of tasks the child has already mastered. In such cases, you might say to the teacher, "Sam can do long division, but gets bogged down if he has to do fifty problems a night. Would it be possible for him to do every other problem, or half the problems and use the extra time for a project?"

And then there's drudgery. Every exciting subject has underpinnings of drudgery. Neurosurgeons had to memorize anatomy; astrophysicists learned formulae. Acquiring this knowledge is an unavoidable drudgery, and not all homework can be fun. Your child needs to learn and rehearse facts and procedures. The need for solid foundations requires that your child will have to do some memorization, repetition, and intellectual setting-up exercises. That's life.

11. Does your child have the prerequisite reading skills to manage assigned homework?

In order to know whether your child has the prerequisite reading skills for the assigned homework, you need to understand how reading prowess unfolds.

Reading levels progress this way:

Emergent reading: understanding what reading is, recognizing a few words

Early reading: being able to sound out words or string words together in short sentences

Con'-tent reading: getting information and plot from reading

Con-tent' reading: relaxed, accurate intake; fluency; use of punctuation for phrasing

Nimble reading: moving easily among factual, survey, and aesthetic reading

In grades three to five, most children incorporate the first three reading levels as they move into, and master, the final two.

Students in these grades move from "learning to read" to "reading to learn." In order to do that, they need the prerequisite reading skills listed below:

- The ability to recognize some words by sight

- The abilty to decode words (sound them out)

- The ability to encode words (spell them)

- The ability to transcode words (convert words and sentences into meaning)

As a parent, you must *be sure* your child's reading skills are in good repair. If you have any concerns about this, request individual testing through the school system or get testing on your own. If your child is at or below grade level on standardized reading testing, get more information now. If there are holes in her skills, get help to plug them up now. Don't wait. Things will not improve spontaneously. Troubles will multiply and minor lapses may turn into major catastrophes.

Sad to say, many children whose early reading instruction didn't stick arrive in grades three to five as fake readers. They know some sight words, they understand bits and pieces of phonics, they have some shaky comprehension strategies, but they are walking on quicksand. If they can't read the text, they can't do the homework. Smiles and good attitude aren't enough. Skills matter.

12. Do your child's developmental and language levels match the assigned tasks?

You can't make the grass grow by pulling it. In fact, you risk yanking it out. The same idea applies to children's developmental levels, not simply in early childhood but all the way to adulthood. Actually, common knowledge now tells us that adults have their developmental progressions, too.

To be successful, academic tasks must match the learner's developmental level. Kids show us when they are developmentally overwhelmed. We just need to learn to read the signals correctly. In wise, pithy words, Anthony Bashir, a Boston-based professor and linguist, illustrates this in saying, "When we give children tasks beyond their developmental level, they punish us by showing us how dumb they are."

Children tell us a great deal about their developmental level by their humor and their literary appetites. For example, most students in grades three to five relish puns, the cornier the better. They also enjoy exploring cause and effect, and, unless they have been schooled out of it, they enjoy questions that don't have correct answers listed in the back of the book. For this reason, mythology has great appeal: origins of the first bubble, or rainbow, or, to cite Kipling's *Jungle Books,* where did the elephant get its trunk? They like to amass facts with which to stump their peers, siblings . . . and *parents!*

Most students this age are not ready to write twenty-page papers! While outlining and webbing, sometimes called mind-mapping, are appropriate skills to learn at this age, and are good foundations for later work, that doesn't mean these students should be expected to do the later work earlier. They should use their skills at their own level.

Understanding the combination of developmental appetites and language levels allows parents and teachers to coordinate homework and reading assignments with the child's natural interest levels and capacities. Bingo!

In the language domain, between grades three and five, most children can make a concise definition: a sofa is a piece of furniture, a lake is a body of water, afraid is a bad feeling. Why do we care? The ability to make a definition represents the ability to sort out the most important facts from a whole collection of associations: I can sit on

Be on the lookout for the problem of "raise the bar and blame the kid." As current culture clamors for educational reform and heightened standards, some kids are getting caught in a nasty pinch. The school (or an individual teacher) decides to notch up the requirements without providing the necessary skills to perform the task. An example of this was the fifth-grade teacher who announced that from that time on, all tests would contain only essay questions. However, her students didn't know how to write essays. She showed them once, but that's not enough. Teachers must teach the skills they require, they must give students opportunities to practice, and they must offer feedback. If your child is in this predicament, you can talk to the teacher about this specific problem, try to teach the skill yourself, or talk to the administrator of your child's division in school about the discontinuity between expectations and teachings.

my sofa, but the dog isn't supposed to lie there; last week I dropped a piece of pizza, juicy side down, on the sofa and got in trouble; sofas are expensive.

The ability to sift and to retrieve what matters most (the salient feature) also underlies the ability to summarize and to think in hierarchies, and, thus, are prerequisite to higher learning, independent thinking, and, of course, homework. A child who cannot make a definition will struggle with the skills just mentioned.

Practice with your child. Start by giving an example, such as the one about the sofa. Talk about which facts are the most important and which one establishes the general category. Can your child define *pig, boat,* or *house?* Does your child establish the generic category? If not, use simpler examples, model the reasoning, and practice.

Children in grades three to five are ready to learn word derivations. Some don't know that words, like people, have ancestors, cousins, and offspring. You might start with the word *manual,* explaining that it comes from the Latin word *manus,* meaning hand. Brainstorm with your child what other words come from this same root and see if you can figure out what they mean. You will probably generate *manuscript, script* = writing, *manus* = hand, therefore *manuscript* means *handwriting. Tele-* is from the Greek meaning *far.* If that's so, what do the following mean: *television, telephone, telescope?*

Children this age enjoy these puzzles.

At this age, children with normal language development discover that single words can have multiple meanings: *steal/steel* (homonyms), *chart* (verb)/*chart* (noun). This knowledge opens the door to puns. If your child doesn't get these jokes, pay attention. Language and developmental levels support intellectual capacities and social/emotional growth. Kids who don't get the joke, who can't catch the humor on the fly and dish it back quickly, have a hard time being included.

Children in these years need to become familiar with such linguistic devices as passive constructions, embedded clauses, dependent clauses, figures of speech, idiom, and simile.

If you say, "The girl was pushed by the boy," can your child tell who did the pushing?

If you say, "The girl, standing beside the man, was pushed by the boy," is your child sure whether it was the girl or the man who was pushed?

If you say, "The girl, the man's granddaughter, was pushed by the boy," does your child know who got pushed?

If you say, "The girl, a likeness of her grandfather, was pushed by the boy," does your child know what *likeness* means?

If you say, "That boy burned his bridges," does your child know what happened to the boy . . . and why?

If you say, "The girl, as delicate as a wild flower, was pushed by the boy," does your child think the girl was standing in a garden?

13. Do your child's handwriting skills match the task?

Yes, handwriting matters even in the electronic era. By now, it's too late to change your child's pencil grip, so don't waste your energy. But you can encourage him to choose either manuscript or cursive writing, practice it for short spurts regularly, and reward legibility. Ask your child to help you by writing out the shopping or errand list that you dictate. Give a bonus for legibility. Give a double bonus for legibility and tidiness. This is an area where you can help without stepping on teachers' toes. Does handwriting matter? Emphatically, yes. People need it for:

- Taking notes in the lecture after the battery on the laptop dies.

- Taking a phone message.

- Writing a thank-you letter. Kids deserve to know the life truth that people give better birthday presents to kids who write handwritten thank-you letters.

- Writing a love letter . . . and yes, that day will come.

- Getting a job. A recent business publication ran an article titled "How to Nail Down That Really Great Job After the Interview." Suggestion #1: Write a handwritten letter of thanks to your interviewer!

In addition to handwriting, help your kid develop accurate keyboard fingering. These are the ideal years to accomplish this task.

14. Do your child's study skills and learning styles match the assigned tasks?

Here are five ways you can help your child build solid study skills:

1) For children this age, you and/or the teacher should create a homework checklist of what's to be done and when each assignment is due. Ideally, this checklist will live in your child's binder.

2) Be sure the Time and Space Pact is in good working order.

3) Your child needs to be familiar with methods for note-taking, outlining, and highlighting. If she is expected to study from notes taken in class (from the chalkboard or from oral presentations), she needs to become an effective note-taker. Volunteer to look over your child's notes and encourage your

child to ask the teacher for help and practice until this increasingly vital skill is solid.

4) Does your child understand and use the appropriate conventions for three different kinds of reading: factual, survey, and aesthetic? Factual reading must be accurate and is often nitpickingly slow. Survey reading requires the ability to skim and zoom in on vital information. Aesthetic reading requires the ability to understand imagery, lose oneself in a story, identify with characters or periods of time, and hear the music of the words. Often, simple recognition of these distinctions brings spontaneous improvement.

5) Use television with your child to practice summarizing and predicting.

In addition to these concrete study skills, you need to understand your child's learning styles so you can measure the "goodness of fit" between *how* your child learns and *what* she is being asked to do. Just as each person has a unique and permanent fingerprint, each person has an individual learning style.

Learning styles show early, though of course children change and develop new skills as they mature. For this reason, it is silly to say of a ten-year-old, "Tony is an auditory learner." Pigeonholing is dangerous as well as foolish. Your child may show different styles and patterns in different settings and for different requirements. That said, I will also say from experience and from the research that dyslexia, learning dis- abilities, some kinds of giftedness (academic and other types), and proclivities send up their flags in young children. We need to be good interpreters.

Academic giftedness makes children chafe at pedantry, dullness, and repetition. These children need to be able to make connections between what they are learning in school, the outside world, and their imaginations. Potentially, homework is an ideal vehicle. Children who are gifted need time and opportunity to refine their talents as well as to trot in harness with their classmates. Homework can be a glorious opportunity.

Dreamers may need to sharpen up. Those who drift may be showing signs of ADD/ADHD (Attention Deficit Disorder/Attention Deficit with Hyperactivity Disorder). These terms are fashionable right now and may be seriously overused. However, when the condition is real, it is really real. If you suspect this in your child, you may want to consult a neurologist or a psychiatrist.

Some children are both gifted *and* dyslexic or learning disabled. They have particular but manageable needs. Parents and educators need to help them in their areas of need and provide scope and exercise for talents. Unsupported weaknesses ache; unexercised talents itch. Parents need to budget time, money, and psychological and emotional resources accordingly, remembering that there is life after school, both now and in the long run.

Children who aren't gifted or learning disabled also possess different learning styles. For example, tempo varies widely among children this age. Some quick students zoom through concepts and work. Others like to spend lots of time on topics that interest them. Slower children may plod along or, taking only a surface view, skim through and overlook important aspects.

Some learners like to receive small bits of information and then string those together into a concept. They are called *sequential* learners. Others need to see the big overall picture first, then they can break it down into its components, reassembling them into the whole. They are called *simultaneous* learners. These distinctions play a big role in children this age. Simultaneous learners may need to see an outline and illustrations of a concept first or hear the names of the characters before trying to follow a plot. Trouble follows if a sequential learner has a freewheeling simultaneous teacher or a simultaneous student has a "one foot in front of the other" teacher.

When teaching style and learning style are markedly different, the resulting discomfort can be as intense as that of wearing an unlined jacket of Harris tweed over a new, deep sunburn.

15. What if your child has dyslexia or a learning disability?

Many children who are good in math and science, who are skillful with their hands and show spatial awareness in their skill on the athletic field, in the art room, or in their ability to build and fix machinery, and who function particularly well in three-dimensional areas, may have weakness on the other side of the coin: the two-dimensional realms such as reading, writing, spelling, word problems in math, and organization of written work. Adults need to be aware of this discrepancy so as to recognize its legitimacy when it appears and get appropriate help for the child.

Children who are weak, clumsy, or unenthusiastic readers by this age should be screened for dyslexia, a condition in which normal to above-average intelligence combines with difficulty in reading and writing. If dyslexia is present, the sooner it is caught the sooner remedies can go to work. Get a tutor if strong, frequent, and consistent help is not available within the school.

Children with diagnosed learning disabilities can learn when taught with appropriate methods and materials. The guiding principle is to break down the tasks into small, manageable bites.

A good resource for information, literature, and conferences is The International Dyslexia Association (I.D.A.), 8600 LaSalle Rd., 382 Chester Building, Baltimore, MD 21286-2044, 410-296-0232.

An attuned parent is the best diagnostician on the planet. If you feel uneasy about your child, if you sense your child is different, if you wake up in the middle of the night with the return of an uneasy feeling, seek professional advice. This will not brand you as a worrywart, you will not be making a problem where none exists, and you will not risk labeling your child.

If your child is, in fact, different, if your child is dyslexic, or has trouble with attention, the sooner it's out in the open the better. If the condition remains a private worry, secret fretting will drain your energies. By seeking a diagnosis, you will air the problem. The word may come back that you were right to worry. Fine. Now you can get going with remedies. If everything is normal, you will have disposed of unnecessary emotional baggage. It's never too early to worry and it's never too late to help.

In the meantime, lobby for as many hands-on projects as possible. Let's say your child, who loves projects but has a hard time with writing, is asked to do a book report. Check with the teacher to see whether your child can make a five-panel storyboard of the book, complete with captions for each section. Or see whether the book report could be in the form of a diorama (made in a shoe box with scenery and people constructed of paper and clay) with an explanatory card stating title, author, main characters, and setting. That's lots of creativity, evidence of comprehension, and very little writing. And then, by the way, your child needs to get some writing help and practice, too.

16. Are your child's emotional habits and considerations taken into account?

The emotional climate of your child's homework time can set the stage for enjoyment and success or for discouragement and self-doubt. With your help, your child should be encouraged to verbalize pride or discouragement in what he has done. You need to listen, rephrase, and reinterpret to be sure everyone is on the same page. Then you can solve problems with words and model constructive behavior.

People of all ages develop emotional habits just as they learn physical habits. Through the experiences you orchestrate and your responses to your child's successes or failures, you play a huge role in the development of optimism and pessimism. Of course some determination is genetic, but nurture is powerful.

Emotional predisposition to optimism or pessimism stacks the deck in favor of success or failure. If there is something your child cannot manage, you can say, "Let's see how we can break this down in little bits, then we'll be able to do it," or "Let's figure out what was going right, and then see what went wrong. That way we can figure it out."

These aren't just "have a nice day" ideas or things I've thought up on my own. Research and wisdom together show that children flourish when they are encouraged to try new things, make mistakes, and learn from them. From among many leaders in child development, I've chosen three of my favorites to illustrate this point.

Erik Erikson, revered figure in the fields of psychoanalysis and human development, said that school-age children internalize the generalization, "I am what I can make work." Children equate their worthiness (of parental love) with how they view themselves as students. Adults need to give them things they can make work.

My own work led me into the neuropsychological research on the limbic system, the emotional brain. This particular "mission control" has the power either to open or to close doorways and pathways to learning and memory. Frightened, embarrassed, humiliated and/or ashamed kids don't learn new information well. They also lose access to facts and information they already know. The emotional climate of the home and the classroom is in the hands of parents and teachers, and maintaining an atmosphere of trust, in which it is permissible to take a chance on an idea without fear of ridicule, is one of the most sacred trusts adults have.

Martin E.P. Seligman, author and professor of psychology at the University of Pennsylvania, demonstrates that children develop feelings of "learned helplessness" or "learned competence" depending on the outcome of their attempts. Those who tend to learned helplessness cave in at the prospect of new or hard things and give up quickly in the face of discouragement. Those inclined to learned competence tackle challenges with gusto as though sipping from internal wells of Gatorade or eating "bowls of courage."

Several years ago, a child entered third grade in our school in mid-November. Swedish by upbringing, his English was school-taught but not spontaneous. I wanted to know where to begin my teaching, so I gave him some tests, but I wanted something more personal. I asked him if he knew the story of *Goldilocks and the Three Bears*, and if he would tell it to me. As often happens when people are learning a new language, they mix up words that sound alike.

This little boy started telling me about "the little girl with yellow hair." He told me about her finding the house in the woods, and what happened when she tried the beds and the chairs. Then he said, "She went into the kitchen and there she found three bowls of 'courage.' The first bowl was too hot and it burned her mouth. The second bowl was too cold and had lumps, but the third bowl was just right, and so she ate the whole thing."

You can help your child find just the right bowl of courage, warm and tempting, an offering that will stick to the ribs and provide long-lasting nourishment. How?

First, the simple-sounding ideas in this book are the ingredients of satisfying work and sustenance. Second, consciously acknowledge the role and power of emotions. They are not "extras," they are foundations. Probably you have sensed this intuitively; now you have scientific and clinical validation. Trust it.

We know from a number of studies that it is between grades three and five that children make the unconscious decision of whether to remain in school or to drop out. If your child feels supported and optimistic—even if the work is hard—he will make the deep-down decision to hang in and do the job. You can influence that decision.

A major goal of homework at this age should be competence and success. These bloom when your child recognizes and acknowledges new competencies. Ask your child to say out loud, "What can I do, understand, and manipulate now that I couldn't before in math? Science? Computer? Language arts? Art? Sports?" Have your child go through the list and verbalize his responses.

At this age, the payoff of homework should be review of skills; opportunities to ruminate and blend new information with old; chances to exercise imagination through writing, art, or projects; and developing ways to integrate computer efforts with the above. Remember, however, the difference between downloading and deliberating. The former is finger exercise, the latter is mental exercise. Discuss this difference with your child.

Parents often ask me how to build motivation. It's not hard. Motivation springs from confidence. Confidence is the natural flower of competence. Whether it is finding the sweet spot in tennis or learning how to spell a four-syllable word, be sure that your child is learning new competencies, and has opportunities to showcase and demonstrate them. You are an ideal audience. These bring confidence, which brings motivation.

17. Do your child's memory skills match the expectations of the homework?

Memory's four main jobs are to:

- put things in

- file things as efficiently and as accurately as possible

- retrieve things as efficiently and accurately as possible

- use memories in combination with new things to make novel connections

The ability to lodge facts, emotions, concepts, and ideas in memory is enhanced by a benevolent emotional climate, physical well being (sufficient sleep, nourishment, and bodily comfort), and a "goodness of fit" between the developmental, language, and reading levels of the student and the materials. The opposites weaken all types of memory capacities. Let's consider two different varieties of memory, and then explore what you can do to help build your child's memory skills.

Short-term memory is just what the name implies: healthy people can remember what they did this morning, or an hour ago. Activities and intelligible information go in and stick for a short while. During this time, they are available for retrieval and for use.

Long-term memory is also what the name implies. Our minds and our brains transfer some items into long-term storage, available for retrieval now and for decades to come. For example, I visited an Alzheimer's patient today. This man in his eighties is unable to remember the name of the person who has taken care of him for six months, but he can tell you every detail of the winning baseball game he pitched in college.

The trick of memory lies in moving information from the short term into long-term storage. In grades three to five, the memory demands on your child might include spelling rules; the multiplication tables; some historical dates, people, and events; procedural steps for the computer; what time lunch happens; people's names; and where to line up to get on the right bus to go home.

In order to get items into long-term storage, people of all ages need to understand what they are doing as they go along. Your child probably will not absorb vocabulary words she doesn't understand, and she cannot "remember" what hasn't gotten in to start with.

How can you help your child? A three-part glue helps things stick. The glue recipe is:

1) Create a benevolent emotional climate in which intellectual/conceptual risk is safe.

2) Join hands-on physical experience with the event or information.

3) Attach language to the event or information.

We know that multisensory teaching (which combines visual, auditory, kinesthetic, and tactile) helps children remember. When a child in grades three to five writes out a piece of information, sees it, hears it, says it, and writes it, the information is apt to stick.

Memory studies, common sense, and personal experience all teach us to learn small bits first, and then connect them. Along the same lines, three short practices produce better results than one long one. If your child is memorizing lines for a play, have her learn a few sets of responses, and then integrate them into the whole scene. If your child needs to learn a speech by heart, take the same approach: learn six or eight lines at a time.

There are some helpful strategies for memorizing factual information, a prime one being acronyms. I can remember the names of the five Great Lakes because of HOMES: Huron, Ontario, Michigan, Erie and Superior. If your child needs to commit something to memory, encourage her to invent an acronym.

You can also show your child how to set factual information to music. Lyrics are easier to remember than dry, disconnected facts. For example, if your child has trouble learning the multiplication tables, set them to familiar tunes. The seven table fits nicely to "Oh My Darling Clementine": Seven ones they come to seven, seven twos are four-or-teen, seven threes are twenty-one, seven fours are twenty-eight.

Apart from homework, you can also offer your child practice in retrieving and combining. Exercising this kind of thinking pays big dividends in general cognitive development. An example might be, "How do you think tonight's basketball game was similar to last week's? How was it different? Has the team changed since last year?"

18. Does the homework attach new concepts to ones that are already familiar?

Students can't learn two unfamiliars at the same time. They need the "velcro" of the familiar as a place for new information to stick. A child who has no concept of island or native populations can't learn about "the aborigines of the archipelago."

You can help in the following four ways:

First, help your child put experience into words. Language is one ingredient of the memory glue. This is an ideal way to introduce new vocabulary, by attaching it to the child's actual experiences.

Second, discuss current events—elections, sports, local events, and national figures—so that these names and concepts are part of your child's conceptual equipment.

Third, use television as one of many sources of information. Used wisely, it can be more than cognitive anesthesia. For example, at the end of a program, discuss with your child the main idea or help him summarize the whole story or plot points.

Fourth, tell family stories. Be specific about where and when they happened, what life was like at that time. My grandchildren like to hear about my mother, a diminutive beauty who wore hats with veils and smoked Parliament cigarettes in long white holders. She carried a fur muff and went sledding in high-heeled boots.

In addition to being fun and weaving a rich tapestry of personal family associations, family stories provide historical context, vocabulary, imagery, and emotional identification . . . all of which are the foundations of understanding literature and identifying with various eras in history.

You, as a parent, have the opportunity to bring family stories alive for your child. You are the one to bestow this gift that will be a treasure throughout your child's life and will be passed down to future generations. Do it.

19. Does your child's homework promote privacy, participation, and enjoying your kid?

Your child needs privacy in homework, particularly in writing and in areas where errors are likely. This doesn't mean that mistakes are shameful, just that no one likes to make them in public. Even though your child at this age may be proclaiming independence, he still wants to please you. You can help by being forthright about the mistakes you make and by trying new things in front of—and with—your child. Examples speak louder than words.

Participation gives children a chance to share as much as they want about their current project or reading level and it gives you a chance to delight in burgeoning accomplishments without being nosy. When you are invited to participate, try to offer strategies and techniques rather than answers.

For example, one parent of a fourth grader said, "I won't help you write the paper, but I'll show you a trick I learned from my college professor, Dr. Mayo-Smith. You are going to write about why the town should spend $100,000 on a park instead of on a parking lot. In your first paragraph, say 'Five reasons to use the money on a park are . . . ' Then list and describe them. Write one paragraph apiece on each of the five reasons, justifying them with details. In your concluding paragraph say, 'I have shown five reasons to spend the money on a park. Finally a park would . . . ' and finish the sentence as you wish. This structure works in millions of different situations and gives the reader a clear sense of what's going to happen. Readers like that. I'd be glad to read your paper when it's done or read the paragraphs as you write them. Your choice."

You can also participate by offering to chaperone a field trip or a game, working on makeup for the class play, or volunteering to read aloud to the class.

Perhaps the most important charter you have is to enjoy your kid. This vote of confidence, hard to codify but easy to spot, encourages pride, enjoyment, and energy.

20. Do you watch the "Plimsoll Line"? (No, it's not a new television show.)

"The Plimsoll Line (sometimes called the Plimsoll Mark) is a circle with a horizontal line drawn through it, carried on both sides of all British merchant vessels. It indicates the maximum depth to which a

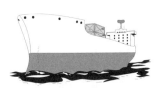

vessel may be loaded, and is named after Samuel Plimsoll (1824-98) . . . who brought about its adoption in view of the great loss of life in overloaded vessels."

—*Brewer's Dictionary of Phrase and Fable*

Overloaded boats are in danger of wallowing or sinking, with possible loss of life. Could there be a better metaphor for homework? Think of your child as a boat with a hull, captain, crew, cargo, home port, and destination. The goal should be buoyancy, safety, and successful journeys.

Well-designed, carefully thought out, and clearly articulated homework can be a welcome oasis of solitude in busy people-packed days, an opportunity to think, dream, wonder, question, and test out original ideas. With understanding and vigilance, your child's Plimsoll Line can be just where it belongs.

Bon voyage!

Priscilla L. Vail, M.A.T.

For more books and materials by Priscilla L. Vail, M.A.T., visit: http://www.priscillavail.com

CHAPTER 1

Developing Good Homework Habits

THE TIME AND SPACE HOMEWORK PACT—a "contract" between you and your child regarding where and when homework will be completed (see Introduction)—is the foundation on which success in schoolwork rests.

This chapter will discuss all the various details—such as time, location, and materials—necessary to make the Homework Pact effective. These details are like the fine print of a contract. However, before we get to all the small points, let's take a look at the Big Picture.

Location, Location, Location

As previously discussed in the Introduction, a good spot to do homework is one where your child can work without any major *good homework location should have adequate lighting as well as an area of flat space where your child can lay out some books and paper.*

distractions. After you agree upon a location where your child will work, give him the opportunity to decorate it with posters, a corkboard with pictures of his friends, or other items that make him feel comfortable, but will not distract him from his homework for a long period of time.

Tools of the Trade

Following is a list of supplies that are helpful to have available in the homework location:

ESSENTIAL SCHOOL ITEMS

Pens

Pencils

Eraser

Paper (ruled and white)

Ruler

Dictionary

Notebooks

NON-ESSENTIAL BUT VERY HELPFUL ITEMS

Glue

Scissors

Markers

Colored paper or posterboard

USEFUL REFERENCE ITEMS

*T*o compute or not to compute? Computer access at home is a nice convenience, but your child's education will not suffer if you don't own one. While students are often taught to use computers in school, there are no homework assignments that require your child to own a home computer. If your child needs access to a computer, many schools and local libraries have computer labs.

Keep in mind that computers can also be a source of distraction. If your child has access to the Internet, she can easily spend several hours on the Web surfing instead of working. You may even want to check in on her occasionally to make sure that there is actual education afoot, and not some fast and furious video game.

Thesaurus

Grammar book

Encyclopedia (CD-ROM version or regular)

Atlas

Certain projects may require additional supplies, which you can purchase on a case-by-case basis.

The reference items listed are definitely useful items to have around, but don't tear your hair out if you don't have them. While it would be great if your child had access to an encyclopedia at your house, she can get by just as easily by using the encyclopedias at the nearest branch library, or the ones at the school library, for that matter.

How to Help Your Child With Hard Facts

Your child's homework assignments will often involve quests for facts. A good approach for this kind of assignment is to set up a series of steps your child should follow before asking for help from you. He should give every question his best shot, skipping over problems that are giving him trouble during his first pass through. Then he should spend some additional time trying to figure out the tough problems on his own, turning to reference books or other resources if necessary. If the extra time and other resources don't help, it's your turn to step in. When you do, remember:

•••••

Telling your child the right answer to a question is not as helpful as teaching him how to find the right answer to a question.

•••••

So if your child asks you to name the oceans, try saying something like, "Let's think about it this way: what reference material could we use to find the answer to this question?" If your child says "dictionary," have him check the dictionary. It turns out many dictionaries do list the five oceans. If your child said "globe," "map," or "encyclopedia," a quick survey of the proper map or encyclopedia page would also yield the correct answer. Using this method, your child learns not only that the names of the oceans are the Atlantic, Pacific, Indian, Arctic, and Antarctic, but also that this kind of information can be found in an atlas, dictionary, or globe. This way, your child learns—and learns how to learn more in the future.

Another way to help your child on fact-based homework assignments is to encourage the use of *mnemonic* (pronounced "nuh–mon–ick") *devices.* Although a mnemonic device sounds like an expensive electronic gadget, it is, in fact, just a tool to help your child remember a certain piece of information. For example, let's say your child's assignment was to look up twenty vocabulary words and write down their definitions. This is a straightforward assignment, but the key is to *understand the goal of the homework assignment.* In this case, the goal is to learn the definitions of the twenty assigned words. If your child just writes down the definitions or doesn't understand a lick of what he's writing, he is going to have trouble when the time comes for him to define the vocabulary words on his own.

Here is where a mnemonic device comes in handy. We can use a word like *squint* as an example. After you tell your child the definition of this word, the two of you can have a "Squint-Down" competition, much like a shootout but less dangerous. Start with your face in a relaxed, normal position. Once one of you says, "Squint!" both sides have to scrunch up their eyes as much as possible. Fastest or goofiest-looking squint wins. Once your child has a couple of rounds of Squint-Down under his belt, remembering the word will be easier. The dictionary definition of squint is "to look with eyes partly closed," and this describes exactly what you do to your face during a round of Squint-Down. Instead of trying to remember a dry dictionary definition, your child can use the mnemonic device of this game to remember the word's meaning. This is much easier to remember, and when the time comes to define *squint* on a test, your child should be able to give its meaning.

Not every word or fact lends itself to a mnemonic device. Some things will just have to be memorized. However, if you encourage your child to come up with mnemonic devices, it should help improve his memory, and it will make basic homework assignments designed to increase your child's base of knowledge more effective.

How to Help with Creative and Long-Term Assignments

An initial hands-off period works well for short, fact-intensive assignments like the vocabulary task described above. However, for longer, more involved homework assignments (a three-page book report) or a creative project (a poster), the opposite is true. Long, involved assignments benefit from proper planning and management of all the various steps needed to complete them, so for these kinds of assignments, sit down with your child before the project begins and help her plan out a good course of action. Once your child has a good idea of what she wants to write about, you can leave her to work on the project on her own. Here are some of the things you should discuss with your child.

Long-Term Project Planning Questions to Ask Your Child

1. In the most precise terms possible, what do you want the final project to be?

When asked to write a three-page paper about dinosaurs, many students just start writing down every fact they can find about dinosaurs until three pages are filled. Instead, help your child develop a precise main idea or topic sentence that she will then write about for three pages. "There are many types of dinosaurs" is a very general statement and not likely to generate a good paper. "The Tyrannosaurus Rex and the Triceratops are two very different kinds of dinosaurs" is a much more precise topic and will probably generate a better paper.

Research papers may not crop up until the fifth grade. It's more likely that your child will be asked to write a short, informative (i.e. fact-based) paper, book report, or creative writing assignment. However, the approach described in the following pages works well for most types of longer projects.

While this example deals with a fact-based paper, having a clear goal works for most long-term projects. For example, your child can develop a precise focus for an assignment that requires her to make a poster illustrating her favorite holiday. The idea "The poster will have something to do with Thanksgiving" is not very clear, but "The poster will show the three reasons why Thanksgiving is my favorite holiday" is much more precise.

2. Now that you have a clear idea of what you want to accomplish, what are the steps you need to take?

The purpose of this question is to help your child break down a large project into a series of manageable tasks so she doesn't become overwhelmed. It is difficult for most people to sit down and write three pages about dinosaurs from start to finish. It is much easier to write a single introductory paragraph, then a paragraph about the characteristics of a Tyrannosaurus Rex, followed by a paragraph on the charac-

uestions related to this general topic also include: How many steps are there in all? What is the easiest step? What is the toughest?

teristics of a Triceratops, then a paragraph discussing their differences, and so on.

By discussing and delineating the various stages needed to complete a project, you help your child transform a large, seemingly impossible assignment into a series of readily achievable steps. Breaking a project down into specific tasks also gives your child the flexibility to work on small pieces of the project over a period of days before the finished product is due.

3. Will you need special materials for any part of your project?

Once your child has laid out all the various steps, she needs to decide what tools and supplies she will need to accomplish each stage of the project. If you do not have these materials around the home, then it is time to add another step to the project, called "Gather Necessary Materials."

4. Roughly how long will each step of the project take?

All too often, students sit down the night before a project is due, only to realize there is no way they can complete it without bending time and space.

If your child takes into account the time needed to finish each step before starting the project, she should be able to get a good idea of when she needs to start working on it. (Since many third- and fourth-grade children are still developing a concept of time, you'll probably need to help her figure out if the amount of time she's set aside for each step is accurate.) If possible, add time to the end of the project to give her some wiggle room, since you never know whether or not one section of the project is going to take longer than it should.

You now have a good method of approach for straightforward assignments as well as longer projects. Many assignments are a combination of these two extremes. If your child likes to attempt most assignments without your help at first, that's fine, as it promotes her personal educational development. If your child needs some encouragement before working, by all means give it to her.

Communicating with Your Child's Teacher

Up to now, we have been focusing on the importance of your role and your child's role in successful homework completion. As previously discussed, there is another person who plays an important homework role: your child's teacher (see pages 8-9). Establishing a good working relationship with your kid's teachers is vital. This does not mean that you should be calling the school every afternoon for a conference. Instead, the main goal between you and a teacher should be coordination. The better you understand what the teacher's goals are for your child, the better you will be able to help him when he does his homework in that subject.

What if You Get Stumped by Your Child's Homework?

It is bound to happen one day. Your child will ask you a question or show you a homework problem that you can't even understand, much less answer. There are two main reasons for this: first, it has been years since you were in grade school, and you just forgot a few things that are important for school work but not often used in everyday life. Second, the terms you used in school are not always the same ones your child is learning. For example, you wouldn't think a word like *subtract* would ever go out of style, but in some areas this word has been replaced by synonyms like *reduce* or *lessen*.

This book is designed to lessen the likelihood that you will be caught flatfooted by your child's homework. We will cover the new terminology used in your child's courses and offer you a basic review of grade school math, English, science, and social studies. Since grade level is a factor, many subjects will progress from easier (third-grade level) topics towards harder (fifth-grade level) related topics. However, since each school is a little different, don't be surprised or upset if your fifth-grade child is just now covering a topic that appears to be at the third-grade level in this book. In places where we can't provide all the information we would like on a topic, we will direct you toward helpful homework websites where you and your child can find the information you need (see page 147).

Even after you finish this book, there probably will still be occasions when you can't immediately answer your child's homework questions. When faced with the inevitable stumper, don't worry. Remember, you may have forgotten a few things, but you are still much more experienced than your child at finding the information that you need. You can turn the occasion into a learning experience for yourself and your child as you walk through the steps of tracking down an answer together.

Can You Make Doing Homework an Enjoyable Experience?

*T*ruthfully, very few children will enjoy doing homework. While you can't make homework something your child enjoys, you can help transform it into something your child does not fear, just something that needs to be done to learn the material. Your child won't smile too often while working on homework, but he can learn the material well with your help. The big smiles are reserved for when he takes a test on the subject . . . and aces it.

This is when you'll both feel like Homework Heroes.

CHAPTER 2

A Review of Basic Math Concepts for Grades 3-5

FOLLOWING IS A REVIEW OF major concepts and ideas that are the lynchpins of math at this level: Number Sense and Numeration, Algebra, Geometry and Measurement, and Data Sense and Probability. You will probably be familiar with most of these topics, but you might have forgotten some of the terminology involved. If you refamiliarize yourself with these ideas, you should have the foundation you need to help with any grade school math homework.

Number Sense and Numeration

Whole Numbers

Math is a very precise subject, and you can't answer the question "What is 7 minus 2?" with "Something around 1, I suppose." In grade school, your child might also be given a problem like, "List all the whole numbers between 6 and 9." The term *whole numbers* is used because there are, in fact, an infinite amount of numbers between 6 and 9—for example, there are 6.01, 6½, and 6.00000347, to name just three. A **whole number**, however, is a number that has no fractions or decimals. The correct answer to the question, "List all the whole numbers between 6 and 9," would be, "7 and 8."

Your child will also learn about **consecutive numbers**, which is just a fancy way of saying "following one after the other in order." In math terms, this usually means going from least to greatest. In the question above, 6, 7, 8, and 9 are consecutive whole numbers.

> **B**y fourth or fifth grade your child might be introduced to negative numbers. Negative numbers are whole numbers, too. So −6 and 6 are both whole numbers.

A good way to illustrate these concepts is to use a **number line** like the one below.

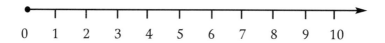

Ask your child to look at the space between 0 and 1 on the number line. That's where all numbers greater than zero, but less than 1, can be found. This includes simple fractions like ½ and ¼. (A discussion of fractions begins on page 52.) All the numbers with dash marks above them are the whole numbers. Have your child place one finger on the 6 and another on the 9—she should now be able to *see* that 7 and 8 are the only whole numbers between 6 and 9.

Math Terms, Part I

Following are some math terms that your child might be introduced to in fourth or fifth grade.

Integers—Any whole number, which includes positive and negative numbers as well as zero. Basically, anything but a fraction or decimal is an integer.

Positive—Any number greater than zero.

Negative—Any number less than zero.

Zero—Neither positive nor negative.

Counting

Learning to read and write numbers up to nine digits long (hundred million) is something your child will learn in the third and fourth grades. At first, this might consist of learning smaller subsets before tackling the entire range.

Learning these numbers is primarily a memorization skill, so you can help by quizzing your child during the course of the day. For example, if your child wants to play at a neighbor's house, you can say, "You can go after you recite all the numbers from 100 to 2,500 by groups of hundreds." Kids love a good challenge, and your child will probably speed through them as quickly as possible. Correct her if she makes any errors and help her if she gets stuck for too long, because you don't want this memory drill to become too difficult.

It is important to get your child comfortable with manipulating numbers in a variety of ways. Giving your child a firm foundation in basic math skills is the main goal of almost all grade school math homework.

Homework Heroics: Counting Practice

IN ADDITION TO simply reciting the numbers, if your child needs extra practice with counting, try having her count thousands by 2s, 5s, and 10s, or count by hundreds up to a certain number.

Place Value

Most adults can look at the number 14,658 and know exactly what that means, but they might have a harder time if someone asked them for the units digit of 14,658. This is a case of grade school terminology that has been left way back in the dusty corner of our minds.

$$14,65\ 8$$

In order to find the units digit, your child must first understand place values. Your child might have had some experience with place values in earlier grades, but at this level he will be expected to know place values up to the ten thousands. The numbers from one to nine have one digit each; numbers from 10 to 99 have two digits. For example, the number 16 has a 1 and a 6. The "6" in the number 16 is in the **units** place (this is also called the **ones** place), and it means there are six 1s. The "1" is in the **tens** place, which means that there is one group of 10. Numbers from 100 to 999 also have a **hundreds** place; in the number 500, "5" stands for five groups of 100. Next is the **thousands** place, which includes numbers from 1,000 to 9,999; the "8" in 8,000 means eight groups of 1,000. After 9,999 you move into the **ten thousands** place (10,000 to 99,999). For the number 41,000, the number "4" means there are four groups of 10,000, and the "1" means that there is one group of 1,000. Now, going back to the example above, your child should be able to tell you that the units digit is 8.

One type of place value question asks your child to change a number into a word. Technically, this could be called switching from the numeric system (1-9) to the alphabetic system (A-Z). Still, "switching from numbers to letters" is probably the best way to explain it to your kid.

To switch from numbers to letters, we will continue to use the place value terminology. Consider the number 8,916. We know that 8 is in the thousands place, 9 is in the hundreds place, 1 is in the tens place, and 6 is the units digit. To write out this number then, we would say:

Eight thousand, nine hundred sixteen = 8,916

When a child writes a number, or speaks the number out loud, they have a tendency to add the word and to the number, such as "Nine thousand and eight hundred and sixteen." While this and is not harmful in any way, it is not the proper way to read the number. Gently encourage your child to leave it out when writing out or speaking a number. This rule is like some of the finer points of grammar: some teachers will let it slide but others won't, so it's best to be prepared for the toughest scenario.

EXAMPLE:
Write out the numeric value of two-thousand six.

Here's a tough question, not for what it contains, but for what it does not. If your child had this as a homework problem, the best approach would be to ask your child leading questions to help him through his place value terminology. For example, you might ask, "What is the value of the thousands digit?" or "What is the value of the hundreds digit?" The only values given are for the thousands place (2) and the units place (6), but if he understands the progression of thousands-hundreds-tens-units, then he will know that in between the 2 in the thousands place and the 6 in the units place, he needs to fill in the hundreds and tens values. Since no value is given, a zero must hold that value's place in each case, so the answer to the question is 2,006.

Adding and Subtracting Multiple-Digit Numbers

The concepts of simple addition (putting two numbers together) and subtraction (taking a number away from another number) are something your child will have learned by the end of second grade. As he progresses from third through fifth grade, he will advance to more complex addition and subtraction of numbers up to five digits. Adding and subtracting multiple-digit numbers is different from basic addition and subtraction because it often involves *regrouping*.

Addition with Regrouping

For addition, regrouping means your child has to "carry" a tens digit. For example,

he first step your child should take when adding or subtracting multiple-digit numbers is to write the numbers in columns and make sure the place values match up (units lined up with units, tens with tens, and so forth). If he doesn't, this means he is trying to answer the problem in his head, and that can lead to mental mistakes. Therefore, take something like

22 + 30 + 8 + 14 = ____ *and make sure to write it out*

        22
        30
         8
      +14
      ____

Notice that the 8 is aligned with the other units digits, not the tens.

Then, your child can proceed accordingly.

EXAMPLE:

        23
      + 49
      ____

Regrouping is needed to find the correct sum for this problem, because when the units digits are added together (3 + 9), the answer is 12, so you need to write down the 2 in the units column and carry the tens digit, 1, over to the left. When adding the tens digits together, it now becomes 2 + 4 + 1 = 7, so the final answer is 72.

Forgetting to carry the 1 is a very common mistake young students make. By not regrouping, they end up with 62 as the answer.

Subtraction with Regrouping

With subtraction, regrouping takes a similar form, although instead of carrying the number over from the units to the tens place, you have to "borrow" from the tens to give to the units.

EXAMPLE:

$$\begin{array}{r} 75 \\ -\ 28 \\ \hline \end{array}$$

Subtracting the units is problematic here because $5 - 8$ gives you a negative number. To fix this, you have to reduce the tens digit, 7, to 6, and then take that borrowed "1" and give it to the units digits, so that "5" becomes "15."

Written out, it would look like

$$\begin{array}{r} 75 \\ -\ 28 \\ \hline \end{array} \qquad \begin{array}{r} {}^{6}\ {}^{15} \\ \cancel{75} \\ -\ 28 \\ \hline \end{array}$$

One way to explain this regrouping movement to your child is to have him think about the number 75 as seven groups of 10 and five 1s. If you take away one of the "10s" and add it to the group of five 1s, what do you get? The answer is "fifteen." Now, instead of 75 being seven 10s and five 1s, it has been shuffled around into six 10s and 15. Numerically, this looks like 70 + 5 = 60 + 15.

This way, the first step of subtraction is now $15 - 8$, which equals 7. The next step is to subtract the tens digits, $6 - 2$, so that the final answer is 47.

Adding and Subtracting Larger Multiple-digit Numbers

Addition and subtraction become a little trickier when you add more digits, simply because there will be more regrouping. A homework question might look like

EXAMPLE:

$$\begin{array}{r} 345 \\ +\ 789 \\ \hline \end{array}$$

This problem isn't necessarily more complex, there's just more of it now. Instead of regrouping once, your child will now have to regroup twice. Adding the units digits, $5 + 9$, makes 14, so the 4 remains and the "1" is carried over to the tens column. There you have $1 + 4 + 8 = 13$, so the 3 remains and the new "1" is carried to the hundreds column. In the hundreds column, you now have 1 + 3 + 7 = 11. If there were more digits, you would have to carry again, but there aren't, so the final answer is 1,134.

Explain to your child that the only difference between one-digit addition and five-digit addition or subtraction is that there are more computations to make, and that means there's a greater chance of making a careless error. However, if he writes his work out neatly and makes sure to carry numbers correctly, then it won't mater if he's adding a nine-digit number with another nine-digit number—he should still be able to solve the problem correctly.

Simple Word Problems

This type of problem is more advanced than the others, because your child will have to first decide what the problem should look like, and then perform the math correctly.

EXAMPLE:

Jonathan has a quarter, two dimes, and a nickel in his piggy bank. How much money does Jonathan have in his piggy bank?

The first step for a word problem is to set up the problem correctly. You can help your child think through this step by asking questions like, "How many coins does Jonathan have in his bank?" There are four in all, because of the two dimes. Your next question would be, "How much is a quarter worth?" then "How much is a dime worth?" and "How many dimes does he have?" and so on. In the end, your child should come up with the equation 25 + 10 + 10 + 5. All that remains is to add the numbers correctly, and the answer is 50 cents.

Multiplication and Division

In grades three to five, your child will learn the times tables through 12 × 12. Learning this type of simple multiplication and division, such as 2 × 3 or 4 ÷ 2, is often just a straight memorization drill.

Your child is given a multiplication or division table, and asked to memorize it.

If this is the case, one way to help your child is to use the techniques discussed on page 45 as a way to quiz your child on the facts. Flashcards are also very helpful when learning multiplication and division.

To multiply numbers larger than 12, your child will again use a form of regrouping. The key difference is that when adding or subtracting, the number being moved is usually a "1": with multiplication, the number carried over may be much larger.

EXAMPLE:

$$79$$
$$\times\ 51$$

In order to do this, you will need to multiply each digit in the **multiplier** (the number on the bottom of the equation) by each digit in the **multiplicand** (the number on the top). So, the first step is to multiply 1 times 9, and then 1 times 7. This gives you

$$\begin{array}{r} 79 \\ \times\ 51 \\ \hline 79 \end{array}$$

Now, since you are multiplying by the 5 in the tens place, there is nothing in the units place. Put a zero in the units spot as a placeholder. The next step is to multiply 5 times 9, which gives you 45. The "5" from 45 is placed underneath the 7 above (next to the zero in the units place). The "4" from 45 is carried over to the next operation, 5 x 7. This gives you 35, plus 4 = 39. So the answer is

$$\begin{array}{r} 79 \\ \times\ 51 \\ \hline 79 \\ +\ 3950 \\ \hline =\quad 4029 \end{array}$$ (The two products, 79 and 3950, are added together.)

Fractions

Most people can recognize a fraction when they see one, but it really helps to understand the idea of fractions completely. To do this, we will use pizza as an example. Seconds after the first pizza slice was created, this fraction explanation followed. (Please feel free to order pizza and follow along.)

EXAMPLE:

The pizza below has been cut into eight slices, and the shaded piece is yours.

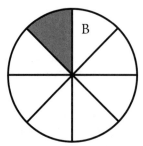

Fractions are used to describe a part of a whole. They are composed of two numbers: the bottom number is the **denominator**, and it shows the total number of pieces in the whole pizza. Since there are eight slices, the denominator is 8. The top number is the **numerator**, and it shows what part of the entire pizza is yours. Since you have one slice, the numerator is 1. Therefore, the fraction that describes your amount of pizza is ⅛.

$$\text{Fractions} = \frac{\text{Numerator}}{\text{Denominator}} = \frac{\text{Part of pizza}}{\text{Whole pizza}} = \frac{1}{8}$$

Let's give you another slice of the pizza, slice B. Does this change the denominator? The answer is no, since the total number of slices in the pizza remains eight. However, the part of the pizza that is yours does change, since you now have two slices. So the numerator becomes 2, and the fraction of the pizza you own is now ⅜.

While $\frac{2}{8}$ is correct, you could also divide the numerator and denominator by 2 and get $\frac{1}{4}$ (this is called **reducing**). This is because $\frac{1}{4}$ and $\frac{2}{8}$ are **equivalent fractions,** meaning that they represent the same numerical value, even though their numerators and denominators are different. To visualize this on the pizza, imagine that your two slices suddenly became one really big slice and that the six remaining slices merged with each other in the same way. You still have the same amount of pizza, but instead of two smaller pieces out of eight smaller pieces, you have one bigger piece out of four.

Math Terms, Part II: Fractions

Equivalent Fraction—Fractions that are equal to each other. For example, $\frac{1}{2}$, $\frac{2}{4}$, $\frac{9}{18}$, and $\frac{345}{690}$ are all equivalent fractions.

Simple Fraction—A fraction whose numerator and denominator cannot be reduced to smaller numbers.

Mixed Number—A mixed number consists of a whole number and a fraction. Examples include 5 $\frac{1}{2}$ and -6 $\frac{1}{2}$. Mixed numbers can also be expressed as improper fractions.

Improper Fraction—A fraction where the numerator is greater than the denominator, as in $\frac{9}{4}$.

To convert an improper fraction to a mixed number, divide the numerator by the denominator. With the fraction $\frac{9}{4}$, 4 divided by 9 equals 2 with a remainder of 1, so the mixed number 2 $\frac{1}{4}$ = $\frac{9}{4}$.

To change a mixed number like 4 $\frac{3}{5}$ into an improper fraction, first multiply the denominator (5) with the whole number (4), and then add the numerator (3) to this number. Since $5 \times 4 = 20$, and $20 + 3 = 23$, the improper fraction $\frac{23}{5}$ = 4 $\frac{3}{5}$.

In general, when giving a fraction as a final answer, your child should use the simplest fraction possible, meaning reduce it to the lowest equivalent fraction. While $\frac{2}{8}$ is correct, it would be better to use $\frac{1}{4}$, since this is the simplest fraction.

To add or subtract fractions:

1) The denominators of both fractions must be the same.

2) If the denominators are not the same, find the lowest common denominator (see below) and create fractions that have the same denominator.

3) Once the denominators are the same, add (or subtract) the numerators only. The denominator stays the same for the answer.

4) If possible, reduce the answer to a simple fraction.

EXAMPLE:

$\frac{3}{8} + \frac{1}{8}$

If your child has to add $\frac{3}{8} + \frac{1}{8}$, she doesn't have to worry about the first two steps, since the denominator is 8 in both cases. $3 + 1 = 4$, so the answer is $\frac{4}{8}$, which can be reduced to $\frac{1}{2}$.

If the denominators are not the same, determine the **lowest common denominator,** which is the smallest number into which both denominators are divisible. Then restate the fractions in terms of the new common denominator.

> **S**tumped on a common denominator? If your child can't think of the least common denominator, she can always multiply the two denominators in the equation together to find a common denominator. She may wind up dealing with some pretty large numbers and have to reduce the fractions she gets as an answer quite a bit, but at least she will get the addition or subtraction right.

EXAMPLE:

$\frac{1}{2} + \frac{1}{4}$

If your child has to add $\frac{1}{2} + \frac{1}{4}$, the solution is easy enough. The first step is to make the denominators of both fractions the same. We can quickly see that 4 is divisible by 2. So $\frac{1}{2}$ can be represented as $\frac{2}{4}$ (remember, both the numerator and the denominator must be multiplied by 2 in order to keep the fraction equivalent). Now, since both denominators are the same, all you have to do is add the numerators: $\frac{2}{4} + \frac{1}{4} = \frac{3}{4}$.

By fifth grade, your child may learn about multiplying and dividing simple fractions.

To multiply fractions:

To multiply fractions, you need only multiply the denominators together and the numerators together.

EXAMPLE:

$\frac{4}{5} \times \frac{3}{8}$

Here, you simply multiply straight across and reduce. So let's take the numerators first:

$4 \times 3 = 12$

Now multiply the denominators:

$5 \times 8 = 40$

We now have the unreduced answer $\frac{12}{40}$. Since 4 can be divided into 12 and 40, we can reduce this fraction to $\frac{3}{10}$, our final answer.

To divide fractions:

1) To divide, you must first flip the fraction you're dividing by (the one after the division sign), so that the numerator becomes the denominator and the denominator becomes the numerator.

2) Then you multiply the two fractions.

EXAMPLE:

$\frac{5}{6} \div \frac{2}{3}$

First, flip $\frac{2}{3}$ to make it $\frac{3}{2}$. Now we have a multiplication problem we can handle just as we did earlier: $\frac{5}{6} \times \frac{3}{2}$. Multiply the numerators:

$5 \times 3 = 15$

Now the denominators:

$6 \times 2 = 12$

The resulting unreduced fraction is $^{15}/_{12}$. This is an improper, unreduced fraction. To get our final answer, we should reduce first. The number 3 divides into the numerator and denominator, giving us a fraction of $^{5}/_{4}$. The number 4 goes into 5 once with a remainder of 1, leaving us with a final answer of 1 $^{1}/_{4}$.

Here's a snappy little ditty to help your child remember how to divide fractions: When dividing, don't ask why, just flip it over and multiply!

Decimals

Like fractions, decimals are a way of talking about a part of a whole, but decimals are based on the number 10.

All numbers to the left of a decimal are for units greater than one, while everything to the right of a decimal is for units that are less than one. We've already talked about place values (see pages 46-47), which covers the numbers to the left of the decimal point. The numbers to the right of the decimal point have a similar terminology, except that there is no units, or ones, place. Therefore, the first number to the right of a decimal is the **tenths** digit, and it means a part of ten. The order then moves to the right (getting smaller the farther away it gets from the decimal) to **hundredths, thousandths,** and so on.

Adding and Subtracting Decimals

Adding and subtracting decimals is the same as adding or subtracting whole numbers (pages 47-50). Just make sure that your child lines up the decimal points properly, so that the correct place values match up.

Multiplying and Dividing Simple Decimals

While addition and subtraction require lining up the decimal points properly, multiplication requires your child to add up the correct number of decimal places properly. A number like 0.8 has only one decimal place (the tenths place), while a number like 0.0437 goes out four decimal places. If your child were to multiply these numbers together, he would multiply the numbers and then move the decimal point over five places—one plus four, the sum of the decimal places—to the left. So 8 × 437 = 3496, and moving the decimal point over five places to the left gives you 0.03496.

For division with decimals, set up the equation first, like

$$0.006 \overline{\smash{)}48.24}$$

Now, the number outside of the divided sign, 0.006, must be converted into a non-decimal. To do this, move the decimal place three spaces to the right . . . *and do the same with the number under the divided sign.*

$$6 \overline{\smash{)}48240}$$

0.006 becomes 6, and 48.24 becomes 48,240. You then proceed with the number crunching.

The Relationship between Decimals and Fractions

Since proper fractions are less than one, the relationship between fractions and decimals is fairly simple. A decimal number like 0.3 means three-tenths, and you can write it $\frac{3}{10}$. If your decimal number extends to the thousandths place, like 0.343, then you would place 343 over 1000, as in $\frac{343}{1000}$. Think of it this way:

• • • • •

However many spaces a decimal number extends to the right,
that's how many zeroes you place after a "1" in the denominator.

• • • • •

To convert a fraction into a decimal, just divide the numerator by the denominator. In grade school your child will probably only be asked to convert simple fractions into decimals. For example, ¼ written in decimal form is 0.25.

Questions involving money often involve decimals. This is because 100 cents = 1 dollar, so if you have two dollars and seventy-three cents, this can easily be expressed as the number 2.73. In the same vein, quarters can be seen as 0.25 dollars, nickels are 0.05, and the lowly penny can be expressed as the decimal number 0.01.

Percents

In fifth grade your child might also learn about percents. The -*cent* in *percent* stands for one hundred, and it is easy to think of **percent** as meaning "out of a hundred." So 73 percent means 73 out of 100, and could be written as the fraction $^{73}/_{100}$. To convert a fraction into a percent, just—here comes some math lingo—convert that fraction into an equivalent fraction with 100 as the denominator, and then the numerator is your percent.

EXAMPLE:

Convert ¼ into a percent.

First, multiply both the numerator and the denominator by 25 to get a denominator of 100. The numerator of this fraction is the percent.

$$(1 \times 25) = 25 \text{ and } (4 \times 25) = 100, \text{ so } {}^{25}/_{100} = 25\%$$

To switch between a percent and a decimal, just multiply the decimal by 100 to get the percent. Therefore, 0.56 becomes 56%, while 0.2 becomes $0.2 \times 100 = 20\%$.

Algebra

Do you remember when you were a small child, and as such, were in a state of continual mock warfare with other kids in your neighborhood? Think back to the time you and your friends were planning the grand assault on your enemies' fortress. (Depending on where you grew up, this fortress might have been a treehouse, equipment shed, sand castle, igloo, or abandoned 1957 Chevy.)

There you were, drawing up plans in the dirt. Of course, you did not have an actual exact figurine of the enemy stronghold, so you just used a large rock instead. The large rock stood for the enemy fortress and everyone understood that, so plans for the attack could move ahead accordingly.

The basic essence of algebra is all about using that big rock and making it stand for something else. In math terms, if you don't know the precise value of a number, you substitute a **variable** (think "rock") —a symbol that stands for an unknown quantity— in its place until its real value can be determined. This variable is usually a letter of the alphabet, written in italics (you most often see x or y).

Selecting the Appropriate Operational Symbol $(+, -, \times, \div)$

While your child will work his way up to solving for the variable, typical algebra assignments in third and fourth grade will probably involve picking the right sign to make an expression true. For example:

EXAMPLE:

Choose the operation that makes this equation correct.

$$9 \ \square \ 2 = 18$$

In a problem like this one, it's not the numbers that are missing, it's the mathematical symbol. Since there are only four operations— add, subtract, multiply, and divide—your child could just start sticking in a symbol and then checking to see if it works. However, this operation can be refined a little bit by first asking, "Is the answer greater than or less than the numbers on the left?" If the answer is *greater*, chances are high that either addition or multiplication are involved, since these operations tend to make numbers larger. In this example, 18 is larger than 9 or 2, so the missing symbol is either or + or × (In this case the answer is ×).

This process doesn't work with all numbers, since fractions and negative numbers can throw things for a loop, but in general it should help your child find the right mathematical operation.

Solving for the Variable

Simple algebra problems provide your child with the equation, and all she has to do is find the exact value of the variable. Harder questions require your child to set up the equation herself, and then solve it.

Now let's try a couple of problems:

EXAMPLE:

Write the missing number in the square that makes the equation correct.

$$3 + \boxed{} = 5$$

If your child is familiar with basic arithmetic, she should be able to get the correct answer on this problem simply by looking at it. However, there is a method that can be taught if the missing number, 2, is not readily recognized as the answer. The key to this method, called *isolating the unknown,* centers around our old friend, the equal sign. Whenever you have an equal sign, it means that both sides of the equation (the left side and the right side) have the same value. Therefore, you can add the same number to or subtract the same number from *both* sides of an equation, and you will still have a true equation. In its simplest form, this means

7 = 7   (certainly true)

7 − 2 = 7 − 2   (the same number, 2, is being
                        subtracted from both sides)

5 = 5   (also true)

Of course, you could add 3 to both sides of 5 = 5, and you would get 8 = 8, which is also true.

Once your child gets comfortable with this idea, go back to the problem. To find the missing piece of the equation, you need to get rid of everything that's on the same side of the equation as the variable. Therefore, you must subtract 3 from both sides of the equation. Now the square is all by itself on one side of the equation, so all you have to do is subtract 3 from 5 on the other side of the equation to get your answer, 2.

$$3 + \square = 5$$
$$3 - 3 + \square = 5 - 3 \text{ (subtracting 3 from both sides)}$$
$$\square = 2$$

If your child is unconvinced, go back to the original problem, substitute a 2 for the square, and determine whether 3 + 2 = 5 is the correct answer.

As your child progresses through grade school she might see a more difficult algebra problem, such as the one below.

EXAMPLE:

$5h - 24 = 2h + 9$. Solve for h.

There are variables and numbers on both sides of the equation. The goal is to get all the variables on one side, and all the numbers on the other, so start by subtracting $2h$ from both sides. This leaves

$5h - 2h - 24 = 2h - 2h + 9$

$3h - 24 = 9$. Now add 24 to both sides to get the numbers over to the right side:

$3h - 24 + 24 = 9 + 24$

$3h = 33$. Divide both sides by 3 to find out $h = 11$.

When a number is being multiplied by a variable, the multiplication sign is commonly dropped. Therefore, 40 $\times$ y or 40(y) will be written as 40y. Division, addition, and subtraction signs are always used.

While this problem has many steps, all you have to do is write down all the work and do the arithmetic properly. The next one requires you to think up the equation yourself.

EXAMPLE:

You have a friend named Kronhorst. You ask Kronhorst how old he is, and he says, "In seven years I'll be 19 years old." How old is Kronhorst now?

This question is more complex than the previous ones, and if your child tried to work out the problem in her head, she could easily get the facts confused.

Encourage your child not to work algebra problems out in her head. The more she writes down, the better her chances are of solving the problem correctly.

The first step, then, is setting up the equation. Since we don't know Kronhorst's current age, we will use the variable q in its place. Kronhorst says he will be 19 in seven years, so we can write this as the equation:

$q + 7 = 19$

$q + 7 - 7 = 19 - 7$ (Subtract 7 from both sides to isolate the variable)

$q = 12$

Math Terms, Part III: Algebra

Following are a few key algebra terms that your child might learn in the fifth grade:

Commutative Property—Addition and multiplication are commutative, because it doesn't matter in which order you add two numbers, or multiply two numbers, the answer will still be the same. Subtraction and division are not commutative. So $4 + 2$ is the same as $2 + 4$, since the answer in each case is 6, but $5 - 3$ is not the same as $3 - 5$, because in the first equation the answer is 2, while in the second equation it is -2.

Associative Property—When an operation appears twice in an equation, if it doesn't matter how you group the terms, it is said to be associative. Addition and multiplication are associative; subtraction and division are not. $(4 \times 2)5$ is the same as $4(2 \times 5)$, since they both equal 40, but $(12 \div 3) \div 4$ equals 1, so it is not the same as $12 \div (3 \div 4)$, which equals 16.

Distributive Property—This property governs how to "distribute" the number on the outside of a set of parentheses to the numbers inside. You can only use this when two functions are involved. So $4(5 + 12) = 4(5) + 4(12)$. You get the same answer because multiplication is distributive over addition. Addition is not distributive over multiplication, since $4 + (5 \times 12)$ does not equal $(4 + 5)(4 + 12)$.

Identity Element—The identity element for any function is the number that leaves other elements in the operation unchanged. For addition, this is 0, since any number plus 0 is that number. For multiplication, the identity element is 1.

Geometry and Measurement

Your child's geometry instruction in grade school will involve learning about lines, angles, and two- and three-dimensional shapes, while measurement will focus on the units of measurement and simple conversion problems, like converting Fahrenheit to Celsius.

Geometry
Lines and Angles

Most basic geometric shapes are created by lines. A **line** is a set of points that extend indefinitely.

The arrows at the ends of line *l* illustrate that line *l* goes on forever in each direction, so there's no way to measure its distance. However, you can measure **line segments**, such as AB, BC, and AC. If AB = 3 and BC = 4, you can easily work out that AC = 7.

To be honest with you, by itself a single line is pretty boring. Time to spice things up by adding more lines!

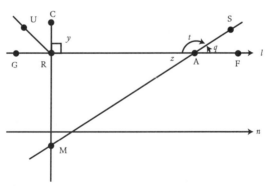

Okay, with this figure we have a number of things to talk about besides line segments. The **intersection** of two lines is the place where

Angle q on page 64 can also be written as ∠SAF, since ∠SAF describes the intersection that creates the angle. Also, while most lines eventually will intersect, parallel lines never do; they are always the same distance apart. In this example, lines l and n are parallel, and this is written l ∥ n.

they cross. The intersection creates an **angle**, such as *q* above.

A **line** measures 180 degrees, or 180°. If you took a line and divided it in half by drawing another line right through the middle of it, how many degrees would you have? The answer is 90°, and the angle that it creates is commonly referred to as a **right angle**; the two lines that meet at a right angle are called **perpendicular lines**. Angle *y* is a right angle, and it is denoted by the upside-down L thingee coming from angle CRA.

Common Angle Terms	Examples
Right angle—any angle that equals 90°.	∠ GRC, ∠ MRA, y
Acute angle—any angle that measures from 0° to less than 90°.	q, ∠MAR
Obtuse angle—any angle greater than 90° but less than 180°.	∠ MAF, t
Supplementary angles—a pair of angles that add up to 180° (straight line).	t and q
Complementary angles—two angles which add up to 90° (right angle).	∠GRU and ∠URC
Vertical angles—two angles lying on opposite sides of two intersecting lines. Vertical angles are always equal.	q and z

Two-dimensional Shapes

Circles

While both you and your child could probably pick a circle out of a police lineup, it is a good idea to be able to define it. A **circle** is a two-dimensional shape in which every point along its edge is the same distance from the center. The circle above has its center at O, and all the points along its edge are the same distance. So line segment OB equals OA, and both of these are equal to OC. If you were to draw in line segment OE, then it would be equal, too.

Now the linear distance from the center of a circle to its edge is called a **radius**, and OB is an example. A line running from one edge of a circle while passing through the center—such as line segment AC—is called the **diameter**. Since this line consists of AO and OC joined together, and since AO and OC are both **radii**, then *the diameter of a circle is always twice its radius.*

Now suppose that the circle here was made out of string. If you were to pick up that string and place it next to a ruler, you would learn the distance around that circle, or the length of the circle's outer boundary. This distance is known as the **circumference** of the circle.

Before we move on to other topics, we need to clear up a couple of terms that get bandied about no matter what geometrical shaped is being discussed: **similar** and **congruent**. These are easy to keep straight:

•••••

Similar figures are alike in shape and proportion, but not size.
Congruent figures are exactly the same size and shape.

•••••

Triangles

Two intersecting lines form an angle, and most of the basic facts about angles are covered in the table on page 65. Three intersecting lines form a **triangle**, a very common geometric shape.

In every triangle, the sum of the three interior angles is always equal to 180°. In Triangle 1, since angle a is **obtuse** (greater than 90°), you know that $b + c$ must be less than 90°, otherwise the sum of all three angles would be greater than 180°. That's bad! In fact, if the figure has more than 180°, it is not worthy of the name triangle at all.

There are three main kinds of triangles that your child will learn about in grade school.

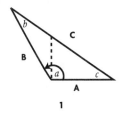

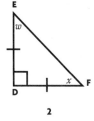

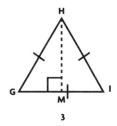

1   2   3

> The dashes in ED and DF are used to show congruency without explicitly writing ED = DF. This is similar to brushing your finger along your upper lip as a way of telling someone they have bread crumbs there—it means the same thing, but you don't state it out loud.

A triangle with two equal sides is known as an **isosceles triangle**. Triangle 2 features two of its sides equal in length. Sides ED and DF are congruent to each other. If two sides of a triangle are equal to each other, then the angles opposite those sides are also equal.

As you can see, Triangle 3 has three dash marks, meaning all three sides are equal. This is called an **equilateral triangle**.

A triangle so ill-mannered as to have no equal sides is called a **scalene triangle**.

Quadrilaterals

Shapes made out of four intersecting lines are all **quadrilaterals**, which literally means "four-sided," but there are some special cases that are known by different names.

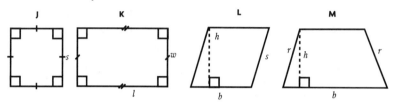

Parallelogram—A parallelogram is a quadrilateral in which opposite sides are parallel and equal in length. Squares, rectangles, and rhombuses are all parallelograms.

Square—The square is a shape with four sides and four corners. All four sides have the same length and opposite sides are parallel. The four corners meet at right angles. Figure J is a square.

Rectangle—The rectangle has four sides, and four corners which all meet in right angles. However, unlike the square, not all sides are of equal length: its opposite sides are of equal length and parallel to each other. Normally, the longer side is called the *length*, while the shorter side is the *width*. Figure K is a rectangle.

Rhombus—A rhombus is like a square that got a little tired and bent over. It is a four-sided figure, and each side is the same length as the others (and its opposite sides are parallel). However, none of the four corners of a rhombus are right angles. Figure L is a rhombus.

Trapezoid—A trapezoid is a quadrilateral that has one pair of parallel sides. Figure M is a trapezoid.

The area and perimeter formulas for several of the figures above are listed in the following chart.

FORMULAS FOR COMMON GEOMETRICAL SHAPES

Shape	Perimeter	Area
Rectangle	2(length+width)	length × width
Triangle	side+side+side	$\frac{1}{2}$ base × height
Parallelogram	side+side+side+side	base × height
Trapezoid	side+side+side+side	$\frac{1}{2}$ height(base1 +base2)

Three-dimensional Shapes

The planar shapes we just talked about are two-dimensional because they have *length* and *width*. Solid shapes are three-dimensional, since they add *height*.

Cube—There are six squares on every cube, and these six sides are called the *faces* of a cube. A cube, then, is a solid with six equal, square faces. Every *edge* of a cube is the same length (your child should be able to see how the sides of each square now form the edges of the cube.) Also, the interior angles of a cube are all right angles.

Sphere—Like the circle, a sphere has no corners, just a continuous curved surface. Remember how each point on the edge of a circle was the same distance from the center of a circle? Well, the same holds true for a sphere, only this time the points along the surface are in three dimensions, not just two.

Cone—Your child shouldn't have any difficulty recognizing this shape, which has a base that is a circle at one end and then tapers to a point at the other end. If your child has never seen a cone before, it's time to break down and take your child out for ice cream.

Manipulation of Figures

Now it's time to start spinning, flipping, and slicing all the basic shapes your child has learned.

Take the rectangle below.

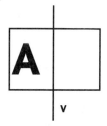

If you were asked to **reflect** this figure across a vertical axis (like V), then you would get this figure:

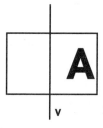

If your child is confused by this, simply take a sheet of scratch paper and draw a large *A* in heavy marker on the left side. Then, keep the right edge of the paper firmly on the table, and lift the left edge of the paper up and over. You should come up with a figure that looks just like the one above. A reflection is nothing more than a mirror image (also called a reverse image) of a figure.

To **rotate** a figure, make sure your child understands degrees and angles (pages 64-65). If you take the original figure and turn it ninety degrees around a fixed point (the bottom left corner of the box, for instance), you get this figure:

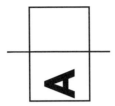

Remember that a right angle is ninety degrees? If you draw the image above directly over the original image, you will see that the two drawings form a right angle. This is because the original was rotated, or spun, ninety degrees to make the second image.

Measurement

By third grade your child will probably have already learned the names of all the various units of measurement, such as time, weight, temperature, and volume. This section will review these elements (discussing both metric and standard units) and explain what each unit measures, as well as provide simple unit conversions, which are the types of homework assignments that your third- to fifth-grade child is likely to receive.

Length

Length is used to measure distance. In the standard system, the basic units of length are

Unit	Meaning
Inch	The smallest unit of length; 1 inch = 1/12 of a foot
Foot	12 inches = 1 foot
Yard	3 feet = 1 yard; 36 inches = 1 yard
Mile	5,280 feet = 1 mile; 1,760 yards = 1 mile

In the metric system, the basic unit of length is the **meter**, which is roughly the same distance as one yard. Here is a breakdown of other lengths. Note that the prefixes are the same throughout the metric system.

Prefix	Meaning	Example
milli-	1/1000	1000 millimeters = 1 meter
centi-	1/100	100 centimeters = 1 meter,
		10 millimeters = 1 centimeter
deci-	1/10	10 decimeters = 1 meter
deka-	10	10 meters = 1 dekameter
hecto-	100	100 meters = 1 hectometer
kilo-	1000	1000 meters = 1 kilometer

On metric conversion problems, everything moves up or down by a factor of 10, so changing units involves either multiplying (or dividing) by 10.

Units of Time

Time is used to measure duration, or how long something lasts. Here are the basic units of time:

The smallest unit of time is the **second**. It should take you about three to four seconds to read the previous sentence.

Unit	Meaning
1 minute	60 seconds
1 hour	60 minutes
1 day	24 hours
1 year	365 days

Actually, the total number of days in a year is about 365.24, which is why we have a leap year roughly every four years. This won't come up in your child's homework, but it's useful to know if your child asks what a leap year is.

A year is also divided into twelve months, which is a period of approximately thirty days. The months of the year are: January, February, March, April, May, June, July, August, September, October, November, and December.

A month can also be split into a smaller unit, called a **week**, which is a period of seven days. The days of the week are: Sunday, Monday, Tuesday, Wednesday, Thursday, Friday, and Saturday. There are roughly 4 weeks in a month, and 52 weeks in every year.

Units of Weight (or Mass)

Weight (or mass) measures how heavy something is. The standard unit of weight is the **pound**. When you have a lot of pounds, 2,000 to be exact, you have a **ton**. (One pound also equals 16 ounces).To give your child an idea of how much a pound weighs, head to the kitchen. If you have any cans of food from a store, the weight is often on the package.

The main unit of mass in the metric system is the **gram**. Based on a gram, your child can then add the metric prefixes on page 72 to increase or decrease mass. The **kilogram**, which equals 2.2 pounds, is a standard by which most things are measured.

Volume (or Capacity)

Volume is the measure of space inside a three-dimensional shape (like a container), so this is the unit of measurement for liquids.

The standard unit for volume is the **gallon**. Milk is often sold in one-gallon containers.

Unit	Meaning
Pint	2 pints = 1 quart
Quart	4 quarts = 1 gallon
Cup	16 cups = 1 gallon; 4 cups = 1 quart
Ounce	128 ounces = 1 gallon; 8 ounces = 1 cup

In the metric system, the base unit for capacity is the **liter**. Prefixes can then be applied as needed.

Temperature

Temperature measures how hot or cold a substance is. The standard scale uses the Fahrenheit scale, while the metric system uses the Celsius scale. In Fahrenheit, water boils at 212 degrees and freezes at 32 degrees (snow day!). In the Celsius scale, 0 degrees is the temperature at which water freezes and 100 degrees is the temperature at which water boils.

Data Analysis and Probability

Data Analysis

Data Analysis usually refers to graphs and visual information, but it also covers number-crunching concepts like mean, median, mode, and range.

Mean

Mean is what most people are referring to when they talk about finding the average of a group of numbers.

EXAMPLE:

If your child had the following quiz scores:

4, 7, 7, 7, 9, 9, 10, 10, 12, 17, 18

what is his mean score?

To find the mean, you would need to add up all the scores, and then divide this number by the number of quizzes.

Mean = (4 + 7+ 7 + 7 + 9 + 9+ 10 + 10 + 12 + 17 + 18)
÷ 11 [quizzes] =
110 ÷ 11 = 10

The mean (average) of the test scores is 10.

Mode

The mode refers to the number that appears most often in a set of numbers.

EXAMPLE:

What is the mode of the quiz scores listed previously?

Since there are three 7s in the quiz scores, the mode of the test scores is 7.

Median

The median can be found by listing all the numbers from least to greatest (this has already been done), and then finding the number that is in the middle.

If there were only ten quiz scores, to find the median you would take the middle two numbers—the fifth and sixth numbers—and then split the difference between them. If you lop off the 18 in the quiz scores, then the middle two numbers are 7 and 9, so the median would be 8.

EXAMPLE:

What is the median score of the scores listed previously?

There are eleven test scores above—we knew that from finding the mean—so if you count over to the sixth number, you will have the number that has five numbers greater than it, and five numbers fewer than it. The median of this group is nine.

Range

The range of a group is merely the smallest and the largest numbers, so the range for this group is 4 to 18.

Graphs and Charts

Mathematical information displayed in a graph or chart (also referred to as a table) provides an added quality that abstract numbers cannot. The visual aspect of graphs and charts—the use of rows and columns to display a set of information—is the allure. Your child will get her fill of graphs and charts in grade school.

EXAMPLE:

Let's say your child went out each morning and counted the number of caterpillars and beetles he found on the elm tree. How would you place the information he gathered in chart form?

Your child's chart might look like this:

Days of the Week	Caterpillars	Beetles
Monday	2	6
Tuesday	3	6
Wednesday	4	2
Thursday	7	4
Friday	8	5

There is the data in an easy-to-read form, but it still lacks a visual element. In order to provide this, let's take this information and place it into a pie graph, a line graph, and a bar graph.

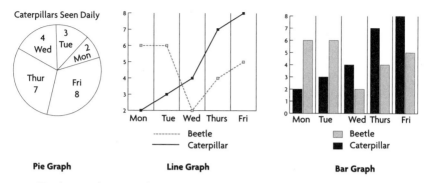

Pie Graph   **Line Graph**   **Bar Graph**

Each graph uses the same information from the chart and displays it in a different way. The **pie graph** shows how many caterpillars were seen each day—it is helpful in showing which days were the best days. Just a quick glance, and your child should be able to discern that Thursday and Friday accounted for the majority of sightings.

The pie is useful to show how each day relates to the entire number of caterpillars seen. If you want to look at how the bug sighting went over time, a **line graph** is very helpful. Looking at the middle graph, you and your child can easily see that caterpillar sightings increased steadily, while beetle sightings dropped during the middle of the week. Line graphs are a good way of showing a pattern developing over time, and while you can compare caterpillar with beetle sighting on it, the **bar graph** does this the best. On this graph, the ability to compare caterpillar to beetle sightings is very distinct. Beetles were ahead early in the week, but caterpillars surged ahead

*I*f your child has trouble reading graphs, make sure that she is paying close attention to the key and the labeling of the horizontal and vertical axes. In the line graph, believing that the dotted line stands for the caterpillar sightings will lead to incorrect answers. Also, getting an accurate number on a graph requires some diligence. For instance, if your child is looking to find the number of beetle sightings on Wednesday, she should go along the horizontal axis until directly over Wednesday, and then head straight up. Once she gets to the right line, she should head straight across to the left to find the number. This is fairly obvious, but sloppy graph reading will lead to inaccurate answers.

later. The difference in amount can be seen each day by comparing the difference in the shaded and outlined bars for each day.

Probability and Odds

Probability problems will probably show in two main forms. Early, third grade probability questions just get your child used to the idea that a given event or outcome is *certain, likely, unlikely, probable,* or another similar word that refers to the likelihood of an event.

EXAMPLE:

You are standing in the Amazon jungle in Brazil. What are the chances that it will snow?
A) very likely
B) probably
C) fairly good
D) very unlikely

At some level, your child needs to realize that it rarely, if ever, snows in the tropics. Therefore, the answer is D.

Once your child gets the hang of likely/not likely probability questions, he will move to the next level. This asks your child to figure out the mathematical odds of something occurring. For example, if, after a million days, it snowed in the Amazon jungle once, the mathematical odds of it snowing there would be *one in a million*, or $\frac{1}{1000000}$. This is the numerical value of answer choice D, *very unlikely*.

Fifth-graders might even face a probability question like:

EXAMPLE:

Nestor has four blue socks, six yellow socks, and eight green socks in a gym bag. If Nestor reaches in without looking and grabs one sock, what are the odds that this sock will be yellow?

To help answer this "odds" question, let us bring back an idea we discussed at the beginning of the chapter: the fraction. An odds questions breaks down to:

Numerator = the number of times the event might occur
Denominator = the total number of outcomes

There are a total of eighteen socks in the the bag, since
4 blue + 6 yellow + 8 green = 18 socks.

So the bottom number, or denominator, will be 18. The top number is six, since this is the number of yellow socks. So $\frac{6}{18}$ is the answer, but this can be simplifed. The odds of picking a yellow sock are $\frac{1}{3}$, or one in three.

CHAPTER 3

A Review of Basic English Concepts for Grades 3-5

ENGLISH—ALSO CALLED ENGLISH LANGUAGE ARTS in some areas of the country—can be broken down into four main subject areas: Grammar, Reading, Literary Analysis, and Writing. In this chapter we will review these fundamental topics and then talk about long-term papers.

Grammar Skills

*I*f a large pharmaceutical company developed a pill that, once swallowed, would give everyone perfect grammar skills, there would be a long line of people waiting at the door with tall glasses of water in their hands (and the authors of this book would be among them).

Homework Heroics: Teaching Kids to Love Reading

THE SINGLE MOST important thing you can do to improve your child's English skills is to encourage your child to read as much as possible. Reading pretty much any kind of book or magazine is better than not reading at all. If your child likes Amelia Bedelia stories, let her read Amelia Bedelia stories; if she likes reading about gophers, by all means get her copies of *Burrow Monthly*. **The more exposure children get to books, the more comfortable they become both with reading and writing.**

Reading provides children with good language models. They see with their eyes and hear in their inner ear (the inner ear you "hear" words with when you read) correctly written sentences put together in moving and interesting ways. This helps your child actually internalize the rules of grammar. She will develop the ability to look at a sentence and determine almost instinctively if it's written correctly, because she knows what correct prose looks like.

A great deal of English grammar contradicts itself; on some levels it's fairly coherent, but on other levels it's seemingly illogical. Here is some advice for both you and your child:

·····

Understand the basics of grammar—subject/verb agreement, proper capitalization and spelling, for example—and look up anything you do not know in a grammar reference book.

·····

Make sure your child has a reputable grammar book on hand— the more exhaustive the better. Once you find a book you and your child like, encourage him to:

1) Use it continuously and aggressively

2) Learn from his mistakes

If you can convince your child to look up grammar rules when- ever he is unsure of the correct rule, you will have made an important step in helping your child. The next step is to get your child to understand his own errors. Here is one way to make sure this happens:

•••••

Maintain a list called "Common Grammar Mistakes," and have your child jot down one or two, along with the correct grammar rule, whenever he receives a rough draft back from you or a final draft back from the teacher with mistakes highlighted.

•••••

Homework Heroics: Be a Good Model

IT MAY BE a pain to mind your grammar when you are just relaxing at home, but if you provide your child with a good spoken language model at all times, you will be doing him a great service. First of all, by speaking grammatically, you help your child internalize the rules of grammar. Secondly, by speaking correctly yourself, you encourage your child to speak correctly, too, which will set him on the road to success in life. Remember your own mother correcting you whenever you said "ain't"? Well, she had the right idea.

English grammar rules evolved over time. The same should happen with your child, with his knowledge of correct grammar being built on a steady succession of mistakes corrected.

Spelling

While some English words sound exactly how they are spelled, there are millions more that do not. Once again, reading can help your child with spelling, since children who have seen the word *cough* written out have a much better chance of spelling it correctly than a child who tries to spell this word from the way it sounds (*koff?*).

Many consonants and vowels show up together in a variety of words, and learning these digraphs and diphthongs can aid your child when spelling. These words sound a lot tougher than their meaning. Basically, both mean "a combination of letters that form a single sound." A **digraph** is a combination of two letters that are used to represent one sound. Some digraphs are: the *ch-*sound in *chin* and the *–ng* sound in *wing*. **Diphthongs** are usually two vowels, or one vowel along with a *w* or a *y*, that combine to form a special combined sound. Examples include the –*oy* in *boy* and the -*ou* sound in *house*.

Frankly, the English language is lousy with digraphs and diphthongs (the underlined letters are just some of them). Unfortunately, learning these letter combinations does not guarantee success, since the same combinations of letters might appear in different words and have different pronunciations. As an example, consider the words *through, ghoul,* and *cough.* Each word has the digraph -*gh* in it, but the combination is pronounced differently in each word.

Of course, the words *through* and *ghoul* both contain the vowels *ou,* and the combination is pronounced the same in both words. This illustrates how learning certain letter combinations can be helpful when spelling an unknown word. Since vowels are more prevalent than consonants, here are some examples of different spellings that go along with short and long vowel sounds.

Vowel	Short Sounds	Examples
A	a, ai, au	bag, plaid, laugh
E	e, ea, a, ai, ay, ie, u, ue	bed, bread, any
I	i, y, e, ie, o, ee, u, ui	fit, guild, busy
O	o, a	dog, false
U	u, o, ou, a, oe, oo	rug, some, flood

Vowel	Long Sounds	Examples
A	a, ai, ay	plane, plain, way
E	e, ea, ee, or ey (if the -*ey* is at the end of a word)	me, neat, fleet, key
I	i, ie, y, igh	mind, lie, why, tight
O	o, oa, oe, ow	zone, boat, toe, row
U	u, ue, oo	muse, true, balloon

Spelling and Syllables

When your child gets ready to spell the word *doghouse*, in effect she is spelling two smaller words and then joining them together to make one larger word (this is called a **compound word**). The word has two distinct syllables, *dog* and *house*. When you see a word like *spoken*, you don't try to say all six letters in one quick rush; instead, you say the first three letters, *spo-*, and then the last three, *-ken*. Pronoucing each syllable, and then thinking about how each syllable could be spelled, can make large words easier to handle. This is easily demonstrated using the Mary Poppins Principle: ask your child to spell *supercalifragilisticexpialidocious*. The prospect seems daunting, but if you go two syllables at a time, your child can come up with a spelling that is reasonably accurate. It is thirty-four letters long, so the chances of spelling it perfectly are fairly low.

The Eight Parts of Speech

All words in the English language can be placed into one of eight categories, so a solid understanding of them is critical. Without further ado . . .

Nouns

A noun names a person, place, thing, or idea in a sentence. *Nutmeg, Mrs. Parkinson, happiness,* and *philosophy* are all examples of nouns.

There are two main categories of nouns: common nouns and proper nouns. A **common noun** represents one or all members of a group of persons, places, or things. *Friend, lake,* and *magazine* are all common nouns. A **proper noun** names a specific member of a common group, so *Lola, Lake Michigan,* and *Highlights* magazine are all proper nouns. Proper nouns are always capitalized.

Pronouns

A pronoun is a word that takes the place of a noun or another pronoun in a sentence. *I, he, we, everyone,* and *several* are examples of pronouns.

A **personal pronoun** takes the place of persons or things. *You, she,* *it, we,* and *them* are examples of personal pronouns. **Possessive pronouns,** such as *my, yours, our,* and *theirs,* show ownership. **Indefinite pronouns** don't substitute for specific nouns, but function as nouns themselves. *All, any, each, everybody, one, somebody,* and *several* are all indefinite pronouns. Some indefinite pronouns, like *everyone, someone, none,* and *each* are singular; others, like *few* and *several,* are plural. Some, maddeningly, can be either depending on the context—*all, most,* and *some* are examples. These pronouns cause students no end of grief when it comes to pronoun agreement.

EXAMPLE:

In the following two sentences, underline the correct pronoun:

Everyone should pack (his/their) own lunch.

Few people I know make (her/their) beds everyday.

When your child sees one of these tricky indefinite pronouns, tell her to be on guard! She must determine if the pronoun is singular or plural before answering a question like this. The only foolproof ways to do this are looking up the answer in a grammar book every time (a cumbersome, but effective, process) or simply memorizing the indefinite pronouns. We recommend the second approach. In the sentences above, *everyone* is a singular indefinite pronoun, so all the other pronouns in the sentence referring to *everyone* should also be singular; that means, "Everyone should pack *his* own lunch." In the second sentence, we see *few,* which is a plural indefinite pronoun; that means "Few people I know make *their* beds every day."

Verbs

Verbs are words that express action, occurrence, or state of being. *Throw, am,* and *laughed* are all verbs. There are two main types of verbs: action verbs and linking verbs. **Action verbs,** as you might expect, express an action that someone or something is taking. "The dog catches the ball" contains the action verb *catches.* A **linking verb** does

*There are some other verb tenses that your child might be exposed to in grade school. The **perfect tense** of a verb indicates an action or condition that was or will be completed before another action or time. Verbs in the perfect tense use a form of the verb to have (I had walked this path as a child). The **progressive tense** of a verb shows an ongoing action in progress at some point in time; it uses some form of the verb to be (I am sleeping).*

not express action; instead, it links the subject with other words that define the subject of the sentence. "Larry is funny" contains the verb *is*, but it does nothing except link the word *Larry* to the word *funny*. Common linking verbs often include a form of the verb *to be*, or are related to the senses (*look, feel*) or a state of being (*seem, become*).

The tense of a verb refers to time and duration of the action. The **simple tense** of a verb indicates that an event is present, past, or future in relation to the speaker:

- Present tense: *I write this book.*

- Past tense: *I ate roast beef yesterday for lunch.*

- Future tense: *I will call my mother tomorrow.*

Most verbs follow the same pattern when changing from present to past tense. For example, the verb *walk* becomes *walked* when transforming from present to past tense. Adding *–ed* or *–d* is fairly common, so *walk* is considered a **regular verb**. Not all verbs are regular, however. The verb *go* transforms into *went* when changing from present to past tense. *Go*, and other verbs like *be*, are known as **irregular verbs**. Your child will simply have to memorize the strange habits of irregular verbs.

Adjectives

Adjectives are words that describe or **modify** a noun or pronoun. The word *modify* means "limits" or "restricts." For example, in the sentence, "That red, four-door car in the parking lot is mine," the adjectives *red* and *four-door* modify the word *car*, limiting the number of cars in the parking lot that could be *mine*. Adjectives usually answer

*T*he words a, an, and the *are a group of adjectives known as* **articles**. *The word the refers to a specific person, place, or thing, so it is usually called a* **definite article**. *The words a or an refer to general nouns, so they are called* **indefinite articles**.

these questions: Which one? What kind? How many? *Red* and *four-door* help answer the question, "Which car is mine?"

Adverbs

Adverbs are words that modify a verb, adjective, or another adverb. Adverbs answer questions like: How? How much? Where? When? Many adverbs are created by taking an adjective and adding *-ly* to it to make an adverb. In the sentence, "The rollercoaster moved quickly," the word *quickly* modifies the word *moved*. In the sentence, "He calls often," *often* describes how frequently he *calls*.

Prepositions

Prepositions are words that usually show the relationship between a noun or pronoun and other words in the sentence. *By, into, on, between*, and *for* are all prepositions. The noun that is combined with a preposition is referred to as the **object of the preposition.** A **prepositional phrase** is made up of a preposition, the object of the preposition, and an adjective or two that modifies the subject of the sentence. So in the sentence, "Your soccer uniform is on the bed," *on* is the preposition, *bed* is the object, and *on the bed* is the prepositional phrase.

Conjunctions

Conjunctions are words used to combine or connect words or groups of words together. *And* and *but* are two of the most common conjunctions. *Or, nor, for*, and *yet* are also common conjunctions.

Interjections

Interjections are words that express excitement and emotion. An exclamation point often separates an interjection from a sentence, but sometimes a comma is used if the emotion's not as strong. In the sentence, "Ouch! That stings," the interjection *ouch* shows it really did sting. Words like *alas*, *yikes*, *hey*, and *wow* are also interjections.

The Four Basic Sentence Types

1. SENTENCE TYPE   **Declarative**

Definition	Declarative sentences make a statement or explain something.
Example	Our town is very pretty.
End With a	Period (.)

2. SENTENCE TYPE   **Interrogative**

Definition	Interrogative sentences ask questions.
Example	Whose book is that?
End With a	Question mark (?)

3. SENTENCE TYPE   **Imperative**

Definition	Imperative sentences give a command or make a request.
Example	Get me a new pair of bowling shoes from the mall.
End With a	Normally, imperative statements end with a period (.). However, if the statement is urgent—*Get these rattlesnakes off of me*!—an exclamation mark (!) may be used.

4. SENTENCE TYPE   **Exclamatory**

Definition	Exclamatory sentences show surprise or strong feeling.
Example	I just won the lottery!
End With an	Exclamation mark (!)

Most sentences are either declarative or interrogative, so your child will be expected to understand the difference between the two and then use the appropriate punctuation mark. With imperative statements, deciding whether or not an exclamation mark or a period should be used is up to the writer, and it depends on the larger context. The imperative sentence, "Bring me some gum," should probably end with a period, but if it occurs within the story, *The Vampire From Space Who Feared Gum*, then the statement might be, "Bring me some gum!"

Once your child has figured out the correct end punctuation, it's time to delve into the sentence itself and deal with punctuation there.

> **S**ince The Vampire From Space Who Feared Gum *is the title of a book, the first letter of each word within the title is capitalized.*

Commas and Apostrophes

Commas and apostrophes are two types of punctuation that your child will have some exposure to by the third grade.

A **comma** is used to indicate a pause and help make a sentence clear. To illustrate this idea, ask your child to repeat this sentence, "It was very very very very difficult for me." As he says it, you can note the slight pause after the first *very's*—everyone pauses a bit there; no one just rushes through and says them jumbled together. There should be a comma wherever the pause occurs, which is why the sentence is correctly written: "It was very, very, very, very difficult for me."

Which came first, the comma or the spoken pause? Who knows? The key is that it's here now, and your child will need to use it at the third- through fifth-grade levels at the following times:

1) In a series of three or more items (hamburgers, French fries, and a milkshake)

2) To separate two or more adjectives (the newest, fastest rollerblades)

3) Between a city and a state written next to each other (Chicago, IL)

4) To set off elements in addresses and names of geographical places (148 Maple Drive, Denver, CO; the train arrived in Miami, FL, early in the morning)

5) Before and after the year when writing a date (May 24, 1990, is the date I was born.)

6) To set off a direct quote in a sentence (My grandmother's favorite saying, "Waste not, want not," always makes my dad roll his eyes.)

There are other rules for using a comma, such as after introductory words in a sentence (Yes, dear) or before the conjunction in a compound sentence, but your child will not need to know these rules yet.

EXAMPLE:

Place commas in the following sentences to make them grammatically correct.:

A. My father was born in St. Louis Missouri.

B. Be sure to bring hammers nails and wrenches to the construction site.

St. Louis is a city in the state of *Missouri,* so be sure to place a comma between those two words. In part B, there is a list of three items: *hammers, nails,* and *wrenches.* Therefore, commas should be placed after *hammers* and *nails,* to set off the items in the list. There's no comma after *wrenches* because the list is over.

Apostrophes are used in contractions and to show possession. Children like shortcuts, so your child should have no trouble understanding the idea behind contractions.

Contractions are a shortcut in English. They are made by joining two words together, using an apostrophe, to make a shorter word. Contractions are most frequently made by joining a word to the word *not* and shortening it to *-n't.* For example, *should not* becomes *shouldn't.*

This seems fairly simple, but there's always something that makes it a little difficult. Certain word groups can't (can not) be contracted,

91

such as changing *am not* to *amn't*. Also, the contraction can sometimes change the first of the two words being joined. Your child might think that *will not* would become *willn't*, but in fact the correct word is *won't*.

That's it for Apostrophe 101. Things get trickier in later grades, since around that time your child will also learn the basics about using apostrophes to show possession.

The verb is can also be shortened to 's and then joined with the word before it. For example, there is can be shortened to there's.

Possession refers to who owns a particular object. An apostrophe is used to show ownership when it is combined with an *s*.

• If only one person has ownership, use *-'s* (Jackie's car).

• If more than one person has ownership, use *-s'* (the twins' card collection).

Apostrophes that show possession are more difficult than contractions for two reasons. First, your child must figure out whether to use *-'s* or *-s'*. Second, *-'s* is also used when contracting the word *is*, so your child must look at an *-'s* and decide whether it is a contraction or if it is showing possession.

EXAMPLE:

Rewrite the following phrases using apostrophes.

A. the hay of the horses

B. the razor of Occam

In part A, who owns the hay? Does it belong to just one horse, or several? Since the hay is for several horses, it should be *the horses' hay*. Only one person owns the razor, though, so it's *Occam's razor*.

If your child looks at the phrase *it's Occam's razor* and understands that the first apostrophe is a contraction and the second one shows possession by one person, then he knows his stuff.

Capitalization

To paraphrase Hamlet, this topic boils down to the question, "To B or not to b?" In other words, when is the uppercase letter used to start a word, and when is the lowercase letter used? Your child will probably already know the three basic rules of capitalization: capitalize the first letter of a word at the beginning of every sentence, when using the pronoun *I,* and when using a specific name (a proper noun).

In grade school your child will also learn to capitalize the first letter of the words for:

1) Geographic names (the Amazon, Phoenix, Antarctica)

2) Holidays (Labor Day, Thanksgiving)

3) Historical periods (the Middle Ages, the Enlightenment)

4) Magazines (*Time* magazine, *Highlights* magazine)

5) Newspapers (*Los Angeles Times, Boston Globe*)

6) Names of organizations (Parent-Teacher Association, Future Business Leaders of America)

7) The first word in a quote (My sister always says, "Live life to the fullest," and I think that's good advice.)

EXAMPLE:

Capitalize the appropriate letters in the following sentences:
Jonas walked up to me and asked me where I was going.
Since jonas is my friend, my answer was, "to bletchley park. Do you want to join me?"

There are four words that need to be capitalized in this question. *Jonas* is a proper noun, referring to a specific person, so the "J" in the second *jonas* needs to be capitalized. In a similar vein, *bletchley park* is a proper noun since it refers to a specific place. He's not going to just any park, it's *Bletchley Park*. Both words start with a capital letter. Finally, the first letter in a word that starts a quotation should be uppercase, so *to* becomes *To*.

Forming Complete Sentences

By third grade your child should understand that a sentence describes a complete idea. In grades three to five, sentence structure homework will probably focus on identifying complete sentences and sentence fragments.

Just to review, every sentence is composed of two parts: the subject and the predicate. The **subject** tells who or what the sentence is about. The **predicate** tells what the subject is or what it does.

Therefore, "my new skateboard" is not a sentence, because there's no predicate. Incomplete sentences are known as **sentence fragments**. If you add "moves very fast," then you have "My new skateboard moves very fast." This is a complete sentence, because it has a subject, *my new skateboard*, that tells what the sentence is about, and a predicate, *moves very fast*, that tells what the subject did.

EXAMPLE:

Which of the following are sentence fragments?

A. Johnny went to the store.

B. Knows few people at school.

C. The science teacher Mr. Klondike.

In order to have a complete sentence, you need to find a subject and a predicate. If either one is missing, it's a fragment. On part A, there is a subject, *Johnny*, that tells who the sentence is about; the predicate, *went to the store*, shows what Johnny did. Complete sentence!

B and C are fragments, since B is missing a subject and C is missing a predicate. If you combine C with B (in that order), you now have a complete sentence.

For more about the various parts of speech that make up a sentence, turn to pages 85-89.

Subject/Verb Agreement

Not only does every sentence have to have a subject and a predicate, but these two items must also get along! The subject of a sentence contains a noun or pronoun, and this noun or pronoun must "agree" with the verb used in the predicate. As seen in the section on verbs, verbs have many tenses and forms (such as singular and plural), and choosing the correct verb for the subject is the essence of subject/verb agreement. Let's use the regular verb *walk* as an example. When referring to yourself in a sentence—by using the pronoun *I*—you would write *I walk*. However, if you are writing about someone else, you would use the pronoun *he* or *she,* and the verb *walk* changes to *he walks* or *she walks*. Therefore, if you wrote *I walks* or *he walk*, you would have incorrect subject/verb agreement, since the correct verbs are not used in either sentence.

Reading and Reading Comprehension

Although there are infinite gradations of understanding, for simplicity's sake we can break reading comprehension into two major levels: basic and advanced. A basic understanding is what your child's teacher will focus on in elementary school, and it means that your child understands the nouns and verbs in any particular sentence. If someone were to say, "Beth owns one thousand spoons," your child would understand that *Beth* is a person, and she would also know the meaning of the words *owns* and *spoons*. An advanced reading comprehension level is the ability to interpret shades of meaning and draw conclusions from information in a text. While your child might do a little bit of this in the fourth and fifth grades, for the most part basic understanding is the key.

Building a Better Vocabulary

Understanding the literal meaning of the words in a sentence is the basic level of reading comprehension, and without it your child will struggle through most English assignments. The main block to this basic level of reading comprehension is an insufficient vocabulary, so by all means

•••••

Make sure your child has access to a dictionary when doing English homework.

•••••

Sometimes kids are reluctant to stop and look up words they don't know because doing so takes extra time, and they would prefer to finish their homework as quickly as possible. It is important that you help your child overcome this reluctance.

Your child's teacher will probably use several methods to help your child learn new words and understand the relationship between words. In addition to asking her to simply memorize the definitions, your child's teacher will spend some time working with synonyms, antonyms, homonyms, homophones, homographs, prefixes, suffixes, and word roots. Once your child is familiar with these concepts, she'll be able to use that knowledge to determine the meanings of words. Below are definitions and examples of these terms, so you can help your child with any assistance she might need:

Synonyms—Words that have the same or almost the same meaning. *Big* and *large, wash* and *cleanse* are pairs of synonyms.

Antonyms—Two words that have opposite or nearly opposite meanings. *Hot* and *cold, near* and *far* are pairs of antonyms.

Homographs—Words that are spelled the same way, but have a different pronunciation and meaning. For example, a *bow* is a decoration you put on a gift, and *bow* is what you do in front of an audience at the end of a play.

Homonyms—Words that sound alike and are spelled the same way but have different meanings. *Park,* as in a nice place to have a picnic, and *park,* as in what you do with your car at the supermarket, are a pair of homonyms.

Homophones—Words that sound alike, but are spelled differently and have different meanings. *Blew* and *blue, principal* and *principle* are pairs of homophones.

Prefixes—A syllable or group of syllables added to the beginning of a word to modify the word or change its meaning. Common prefixes include *un-, in-, anti-, mis-, non-, bi-,* and *de-*. For example, *bi-* means "having two," so a bicycle is a vehicle with two wheels.

Suffixes—A syllable or group of syllables added to the end of a word to modify the word or change its meaning. Common suffixes include *-able, -ible, -ed, -ify,* and *-ment*. The suffix *-ment* means "act or process of," or "state of being," so *merriment* means "being merry."

Word Origins—Many prefixes and suffixes have foreign origins. For example, *tele-* is from a Greek word meaning *far*, so our word *television* really means *far vision*—which is, in fact, what television provides for us. The word part *micro-* is from a Latin word meaning *small*, so the word *microscope* can be defined as *small-seer*.

Many dictionaries have long tables of word parts and their meanings that you should review with your child. You can see, however, that once your child becomes familiar with the meaning of prefixes, word roots, and so forth, she will be able to use that knowledge to break down words into their composite parts to help figure out their definitions.

Homework Heroics: The Shared Parts Games

IF YOU HEAR yourself or your child use a word that has a common word part in it, work together to come up with as many other words that share that word part as you can. For example, if your child says that a particular classmate is "insensitive," try to come up with other words that use the prefix in-. If your child demands that you stop "micromanaging" her, ask her to come up with some other micro- words.

Context and Patterns

Understanding Words from Context

In grade school your child will be taught to use sentence and word context to find the meaning of unknown words. If your child doesn't understand a word in a story or assignment he is reading, try asking him questions to help him focus on the clues surrounding the unknown word. For example: "After eating nothing for the past three days besides some mints he had found in his pockets, the ravenous boy could hardly believe his luck when he stumbled upon a campfire and saw three huge trout roasting on a stick." If your child doesn't know what the word *ravenous* means, you might ask him, "How long had it been since the boy last ate?" "How would you feel if the only thing you'd had to eat during that time were some old mints?" "Why was the boy excited to find the fish?" By asking these types of questions, you can help your child discover that *ravenous* means "extremely hungry."

Identifying Patterns in Informational Text

Third-, fourth-, and fifth-graders spend a lot of time learning how to identify relationship patterns, such as cause and effect, compare and contrast, and sequential or chronological order, to help their reading comprehension skills.

Cause and Effect—This phrase is used to describe how two events are related; the cause is the reason that something happens, while the effect is the result. Let's suppose Milton the Hypothetical Student does no studying for the big math test. Milton then takes the test and fails. These two events are linked, since his lack of studying caused him to do poorly on the test. Failing the test was the effect and not studying was the cause.

Compare and Contrast—Easy comparisons deal with physical objects: how is Car A similar to Car B? (This is a compare question.) How are the two cars different? (This is a contrast question). In Reading, the objects being compared and contrasted are usually not physical. Instead, they are related to the story—"How is this poem similar to another poem?" or "Contrast the emotions of the plumber and the barbarian in the story *Drain Pipe Berserker*." Whether the things being compared are physical objects or not, a good approach is to make two lists, one for each object, and then find the similarities and differences between the lists. Making a list for each object lets your child think about each thing individually, and then work on comparing or contrasting the facts on both lists.

Sequential or Chronological Order—Knowing the order in which events take place is crucial to understanding the events of a story. In *Romeo and Juliet,* Juliet can't die and *then* give her famous balcony speech. (Well, she could, but then it would be more of a zombie story than a timeless romance). Sequential questions will ask your child such things as, "Which event happened last?" If your child doesn't know the order of events in a story, chances are good that he has not understood the story fully.

Literary Analysis

As stated at the beginning of this chapter, encouraging your child to read will help her learn the English language in many ways. Certainly, developing a love for reading will come in handy when she has to create her first book report. Who knows? She might even become the first student to actually read the book, and not just the jacket cover. We're kidding!

But before the book reports start popping up, your child will have to learn the basics of reading comprehension. Simply put, can your child understand not only the meaning of the sentences she reads, but what they mean when combined to form a six- or eight-sentence para-

A paragraph *is a group of unified sentences dealing with one main idea.*

graph or a story with many paragraphs? To do this, she will have to understand things like sequence of events, characters, setting, and some other basic literary concepts.

Common Literary Terms

Here is a sample paragraph of to help illustrate the following key literary terms:

> My family went hiking this weekend. The weather was cold in the morning. In the afternoon it was hot. I ended up sweating up a lot. I was tired by the time I reached the top of the mountain. The view from the top was beautiful. It was definitely worth all the trouble.

Main Idea—Most pieces of writing aren't merely ramblings with no point. They have a main idea, which is the central message of the piece. Understanding the main idea of a story is like providing a frame and canvas for a painting: you still have to fill in all the details, but at least you have an inkling of the overall picture.

Homework Heroics: Summarizing

A GREAT PLACE to find main ideas is a television guide. Local or national, a television guide will summarize the movies and television programs being shown, often in one sentence or two. You can watch a movie or television show with your child, and then ask him to summarize it in his own words. Or, if your child has already seen the movie or program, you can skip the viewing part and just go straight to the main idea stage. This way is faster, but it doesn't involve that favorite pastime: making popcorn.

EXAMPLE:
In the previous story, what was the main idea?

If your child is having trouble finding the main idea, ask him leading questions, such as:

1) What did you feel like after reading the piece? Were you sad, happy, disturbed?

2) Was there a central conflict or event in the story? A moral?

3) Was the story told from a particular point of view? If so, what impact did that point of view have on the meaning of the story?

If he can explain these things, he will be on the right track. As long as your child can back up his version of the main idea with facts or examples from the story, it should stand up well. For example, the main idea in the hiking story above would be something like, "A child climbs up a mountain and finds the view wonderful."

Once your child understands the main idea, he can sometimes makes predictions based on information found in the piece.

EXAMPLE:
Do you think the main character in the story would like
to go hiking again?

By understanding the story, your child can now take a mental leap and make a prediction. This is moving away from focusing on what's written specifically on the page and involves doing some independent thinking, an essential step in terms of literary analysis. The answer to the question above is most likely, "Yes." Your child should come to this conclusion because the character in the story was so impressed with the view from the top.

Plot—Basically, if you can summarize the main events or tell what happens in a story, you have its plot.

If your child has trouble recounting the plot of a particular story, it is probably because he read carelessly or quickly. Ask him to read it again, without outside distractions, and encourage him to make notes of major plot points. If your child frequently has trouble recounting a plot, his basic reading comprehension skills may need work. See our discussion of basic reading comprehension on pages 95-99. If the problem persists, seek help from your child's teacher.

Characters—These are the people and/or creatures within a story. In this nonfiction piece above, the main character is the child. He is the person around whom the action revolves. The main character's family is also mentioned, but they are considered minor, or supporting, characters since they don't play a large role in the piece.

The narrator is the person who is telling the story. Often the narrator is the main character, but this is not always the case.

Setting—The setting is the scenery, location, or period of time in which a story or other work takes place. The mountain is the setting in the hiking story.

Mood—The mood (or tone) is the emotional atmosphere of the story. "It was a dark, windy day" and "the festive party" are examples of how an author uses word choice to establish mood. There can be dark stories about birthday parties and funny stories about prisons—it all depends on the events portrayed and language used.

Simile and Metaphor—Similes and metaphors are figurative uses of language. A **simile** is figurative language in which two essentially unlike things are compared; they often use the words *like* or *as*. "Fit as a fiddle" and "Mohammed Ali floated like a butterfly" are both similes.

A **metaphor** is figurative language in which a word or phrase that ordinarily describes one thing is used to describe another, such as "all the world's a stage." Metaphors can also be a little more drawn out and subtle: "The morning fog lapped at the corners of the street, curled its long, gray tail around its haunches, lingered and licked its paws, then scampered back up to the sky to chase the birds." Here, we can see that

While terms like character, setting, and mood are all helpful ways to analyze a piece of writing, they are by no means the only way. Another good model to try is the "Six Questions" approach: Who, What, When, Where, Why, and How. By asking and answering these six questions, your child will better be able to understand a story. For example, you might ask your child, "Who is the main character?" "What is the central event of the story?" "Why did the character act that way?" and so on.

a cat is used as a metaphor for fog, even though the word "cat" is never specifically used.

Hyperbole and Personification—Hyperbole is an exaggerated claim that can't possibly be true (and isn't meant to be taken as true), but is used for effect. When someone says, "That sandwich was a mile in length," it is a hyperbole. Personification occurs when you give human traits to non-human objects. "The sun is smiling down on us" is an example of personification—huge, fiery orbs of distant matter do not "smile," but people do.

Bear in mind an important rule of literary analysis while working with your child on these kinds of homework assignments:

There is no one right answer in literary analysis. Your child just needs to be able to support his ideas and interpretations logically, using the text in question for support.

This frustrates some children who like definite answers, but try to encourage your child to see analyzing reading material as a chance to be creative.

Major Literary Genres

A discussion of literary genres at the grade school level primarily involves learning how to distinguish the four major categories, or genres (pronounced ZHAN - ruhs): nonfiction, fiction, drama, and poetry. In fifth grade your child might begin analyzing different genres, so we included some tips on the following pages.

Nonfiction

Nonfiction is factual prose writing (**prose** is just writing that is not poetry). News articles, essays, history books, biographies, almanacs, reference materials—everything that is not a play or poem and does not involve making up people, places, and events—is nonfiction.

If your child is asked to analyze a piece of nonfiction and gets stumped, ask her the following questions:

1) What is this piece designed to "do": persuade, inform, entertain?

2) Who was/is the intended audience for this piece? Scientists? Video game fanatics?

3) What kind of support does the author use to bolster his or her arguments?

4) Do you think this piece is effective in doing what it was written to do? Why or why not?

Fiction

Fiction is a class of writing that involves narration in prose form and deals with partly or completely imaginary characters or events. Short stories, novels, fables, and myths are all works of fiction.

When analyzing fiction, one must be comfortable making supportable judgments and assumptions. If your child is having trouble with a fiction analysis assignment, a good starting place, no matter what the required approach, is to look for the main idea and think about the use of major literary devices in the work:

1) What is this piece about?

2) How does it make you feel?

3) What, specifically, makes you feel that way?

4) What use does the author make of figurative language?

See the discussion of literary terms on pages 100-103 and the Six Questions sidebar on page 103 for guidelines.

Drama

Dramas are plays. Your child probably will not read much drama in grade school. Dramas are meant to be performed for audiences, not read, so they tend to be difficult for younger students to handle. However, your child will be expected to identify a play from among other types of writing, so if she sees dialogue and stage directions, this should provide a clue that what she's reading is a play.

Poetry

Poetry is non-prose writing. In grade school, your child will most likely be exposed to poetry that rhymes; in fifth grade she might read a sonnet, which is a fourteen-line poem that has a set pattern of rhyme.

The common literary terms that apply to fiction also apply to poetry (see the discussion on pages 100-103). A lot of meaning can be packed into a few short lines, because the poet makes careful use of **figurative language,** such as metaphors and similes. If your child is asked to interpret a poem, ask her the same kinds of questions you might ask when searching for the main idea and tone of a story.

Writing Skills

On writing assignments, whether they are fiction or nonfiction, you are best off helping your child before he begins, and then letting him write it on his own. In grade school, your child is most likely to encounter one of the following three types of writing assignments:

Creative Writing—Short stories and poems fall into this category. Careful use of language to evoke moods and flesh out characters is important here, but stories need a beginning, middle, and end, so organization is also essential.

Informational (or Expository) Essay—Here, your child will be asked to explain a process or situation, acquaint the reader with a body of knowledge, or describe a problem and its solution. Clarity is key here, so organization will be the main focus.

Persuasive Essay—In this kind of assignment, your child will be asked to choose one side of an argument, make a case for it, anticipate and address potenetial counterarguments, and try to prove that his position is the best one. The key to this assignment is getting your child to clearly state his position and provide supporting evidence that will outweigh any possible alternative arguments.

> *If your child is assigned a multi-step writing assignment, be sure to review the section on Long-Term Project Planning at the beginning of the book (see pages 37-40).*

Writing assignments in grade school vary widely, from a one-paragraph story in third grade, to a book report or informational report in fourth grade, up to a short research report in fifth grade. Regardless of the length of the writing or type of assignment, your child will benefit at any level by following these steps:

Stage One: The Brainstorming Session and Developing a Topic Sentence

It is helpful to begin writing assignments by brainstorming about the project. Help your child let her imagination loose and think freely to come up with ideas for a topic or ideas for approaching an assigned topic. Often, bad or off-the-wall ideas can lead to good ones, so keep the ideas flowing and don't criticize.

After selecting a topic she should refine it into a main idea or topic sentence. Armed with the topic sentence, head onward to Stage Two . . .

Stage Two: Preliminary Research

Note: Your child may skip Stages Two and Three if the assignment is purely creative. If the assignment is nonfiction, your child will

M *ake sure your child writes down the ideas you and she come up with when brainstorming. You don't want to brainstorm ideas one day only to forget what they were the following day.*

likely have to muster some facts. Work with your child to:

Cast a Wide Net at First

Using the card catalog at the library and/or an Internet search engine, you should help your child look up general information about his topic. For example, if he is writing a persuasive essay about recycling, he might want to take a look at some general books on environmentalism first. Then he should do a little preliminary reading with two purposes in mind: (1) To refine and focus his topic to fit the parameters and page length of the assignment. For example, if your child's assignment requires him to write three to five pages, he is going to have some trouble even scratching the surface of a broad topic like environmentalism; (2) To learn of other potential sources that may help him. Most nonfiction books have useful bibliographies and footnotes. Your child should skim these resources for titles of books and articles that focus more specifically on his topic.

Hit the Stacks Again

Armed with a narrow, refined topic sentence, your child should gather sources that specifically address his topic. Here is an important tip no student of any age should forget:

•••••
Ask your librarian for help when you need it!
•••••

Your child should not feel he has to flail about helplessly looking for books. If his search is turning up nothing helpful, he should seek out the librarian for assistance.

Stage Three: Note-taking and Fact Gathering

With an armful of books and articles, your child sits down to figure out what she is going to say on her topic. It is essential that she have some sort of method for keeping track of the information she uncovers for two reasons: (1) It is incredibly frustrating when you can't find a particular fact that you need and (2) she will need her notes organized when it comes time to write a bibliography (see guidelines on page 111).

No-nonsense Note-taking
Encourage your child to follow these steps:

1) Get some note cards.

2) Make a card for each different source, writing down all the publication information in standard form (again, see page 111.)

3) Draw a symbol or identifying mark on each card.

4) As your child reads, if she sees a fact she wants to use or quote, she should take out a new note card, write the symbol for the source and the page number, and then write down the quote, statistic, or any information she wants to use in her paper. She should have a separate, coded note card for each piece of information.

By following this system, your child will keep all her information available and organized. The other benefits of this system will become clear when we discuss rough drafts.

Stage Four: Organization and Outlines

Before your child even thinks about starting to write his paper, he should take some time to organize his thoughts. Learning to present information in a logical sequence, perhaps chronologically or in order of impact, is a focus in grade school.

Two tried-and-true methods for organizing a paper are outlining and mind maps.

Outlines

Outlines are like instructions that help you get through an essay or story without getting confused. Your child's teacher may require him to learn formal outlining procedures. You have probably seen this before. See the outline below, for a review.

Sample Outline

I. A large Roman numeral indicates a large section of a work. For your child, this probably translates into a paragraph. The main topic of the paragraph goes by the numeral.
   A. The main points within the larger sections go next to capital letters.
   B. Write the main points in sentence form.
   C. Here is another main point.
      1. Smaller pieces of information and minor arguments that relate to a particular main point go under that point's letter next to a regular number.
      2. Here's another smaller point.
         a. If you had an even more minor point to make, it would go here, beside a lowercase letter.
         b. Here is another minor point.
            i. If you really wanted to go into fine detail, you can go back to Roman numerals—lowercase this time.
            ii. Here's another very minor point.
II. Second Large Section topic sentence.
   A. Major point.
   B. Major point.
      1. Smaller point
      2. Smaller point
         a. Very small point.

You get the idea. As you move into finer detail, indent and use the next numbering system in the outline.

Mind Maps

Some folks don't like the restrictions of a linear organizational system like an outline. In recent years, an alternative has gained popularity with teachers and students: mind maps. Don't worry, this doesn't involve hypnosis. Mind maps are visual representations of the relationship of the different pieces of an essay. Here is an example:

Sample Mind Map

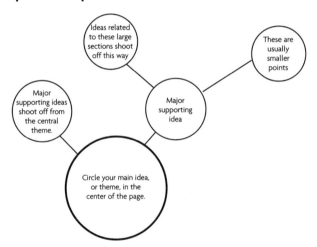

Stage Five: The Rough Draft

If your child has an outline or mind map and all his note cards together, the rough draft should be a snap. He simply needs to go through his notes and organize the cards to follow along with his outline (some tinkering with the outline may occur at this stage, which is fine). If he has taken thorough notes, writing the rough draft becomes a matter of linking the notes with his own thoughts, according to the outline he created. At the rough draft stage, your child should get his ideas or information down on paper; he should focus on putting his ideas in a logical sequence and providing supporting details.

If your child is required to use **parenthetical documentation** or **footnotes**, and a **bibliography** or **list of works** cited, they should be handled during the rough draft stage. When a writer uses material from an outside source in his work, he must provide appropriate documentation of the source. Parenthetical documentation and footnotes are alternative ways of showing the reader of a paper where certain information came from. Footnotes appear at the bottom of a page and parenthetical documentation appears within the text, set off in parentheses. A bibliography or list of works cited provide the publication information for all your child's sources, and it is usually included as a list on a separate page at the end of a paper. Your child's teacher will give him specific guidelines for formatting documentation and bibliographies.

Stage Six: Revising

Learning how to revise one's own writing is a critical life-long skill. If your child asks you for help at this stage, try giving her a list of questions similar to the following ones so that she can try revising on her own first. Afterwards you can look it over and gently make additional suggestions.

Nonfiction

The questions below focus on the important elements of nonfiction writing that your child might be expected to know at this grade level:

1) What is my main idea?

2) Have I established my main idea with a topic sentence?

3) Did I include supporting paragraphs with facts, details, or explanations?

4) Did I conclude with a paragraph that summarizes my points?

If your child is writing a personal narrative, she might ask herself questions that include, "Did I put my story in context?" "Have I developed my narrative with sensory details?" "Did I provide insight into why the incident is memorable to me?"

Fiction

The questions below focus on the important elements of fiction writing that your child might be expected to know in grade school:

1) Did I establish a plot or situation?

2) Have I developed the plot with well-chosen details?

3) Did I describe the setting for my story?

4) Does my story have a beginning, middle, and end?

In addition to revising for clarity, content, and organization, make sure your child does her best to proofread her writing for correct spelling, punctuation, grammar, and usage.

After your child addresses any major problems with her paper, she is done. Ta-da! She can move on to Stage Seven—Turn in Your Paper and Heave a Sigh of Relief. Since the final result is something to be proud of, be certain your child hears your praise for her accomplishment. Good homework habits should always be rewarded, and while most kids prefer cash (credit cards accepted at some locations), words of encouragement are just as important to their psyches.

A Review of Basic Science Concepts for Grades 3-5

THERE'S NO GETTING AROUND IT: science deals with facts. A lot of facts. A lot of facts over a wide variety of topics, ranging from the food chain to earthquakes. What follows is a review of the major concepts that are the foundation of grade school science: Physical Science, Life Sciences, Earth Science and Space Sciences.

Physical Science

Physical science talks about the laws that govern the structure of the universe, such as the properties of matter, motion, and energy, as well the interaction between them.

Matter

Matter is just a scientific way of saying *stuff.* If you really want to be scientific about it, matter is any substance that occupies space and has weight. So a love letter has substance, but love itself does not. Which is to say that love does matter, but it isn't matter.

States of Matter

There are three main states of matter:

Solid—Matter in solid form holds its own shape and has a definite volume. These molecules don't move around freely—but they do vibrate slightly—because the strong forces between particles hold them in place. If molecules are heated, they will vibrate faster and eventually move farther apart.

Liquid—A liquid has a definite volume but no fixed shape. The forces between the particles are weaker than a solid, so the molecules move around and assume the shape of the container they are in.

Gas—A gas is matter that has no definite shape or volume. The molecules are very far apart, so they move about randomly and expand to fill any container into which they are put.

You should be aware of the key phrase, *depending on temperature and pressure.* If you mess with these two items, you can change the state of matter.

EXAMPLE:

By what process can you convert water into a gas? By what process can you convert it into a solid?

The answer to this question is based on common experience. To convert water to gas, heat it to the boiling point. At that point, it starts

*T*echnically, the term gas in the example should be replaced by vapor. This is the difference between a gas and a vapor: A gaseous element exists as a gas at normal temperature and pressure, such as the oxygen in the air. A vapor is an element that has been transformed into a gas by the exertion of unusual temperature or pressure on it. Steam is a good example of vapor.

to become steam or vapor, the gaseous form of water. The temperature is the key factor here. Heat speeds up the molecules' movement and gets them bouncing around randomly like a gas. To convert water to a solid, temperature is again key. If you took water and placed it into your freezer, you would exert a different kind of temperature on it. This changes liquid water into ice, a solid. The principle is much the same with other sorts of matter. Rock can become hot liquid magma spewing out of a volcano if it is heated to the right temperature (thankfully, your child can't try this experiment on your stovetop). If chilled to the right temperature, nitrogen (a gas) can become liquid and be used by your doctor to freeze warts off your skin. Air pressure affects the rates of all these processes; the more pressure that's applied, the cooler molecules become.

Matter: Key Terms

Now that we understand matter and its different states, let's talk about the types of matter in the world and the scientific terms used to describe matter:

Atoms—All matter is made of up smaller units called atoms, which are really, really, really small. An atom is the smallest particle of an element that still retains that element's chemical properties. Atoms are composed of a nucleus, protons, neutrons, and electrons.

Elements—An element is a class of matter that cannot be broken down into simpler parts by chemical means; it is a substance that contains only one kind of atom. Some common elements are hydrogen, oxygen, carbon, lead, and mercury.

Chemical Reaction – While elements can't be broken into simpler parts by chemical means, they can be combined into more complex creations via chemical changes. A chemical change, such as burning,

M atter can also undergo a **physical change**, *which is a change in state or appearance, such as a rock that has crumbled into many pieces. A physical change doesn't alter the composition of the substance.*

creates a change in the composition of a substance, causing it to become a new substance with different properties. These changes usually involve the release or absorption of energy. The binding of two atoms of hydrogen with one atom of oxygen is a familiar chemical change that makes water, our beloved H_2O.

Molecules—Tiny structures composed of two or more atoms held together by a bond. Compounds and some elements contain molecules.

You see, the reason you use the phrase, *molecule of water,* is because a molecule of water is a different type of matter than either hydrogen or oxygen. Have you ever noticed that marriage sometimes changes two people? You knew the people when they were single, but now that they've married they're completely different? Well, the same theory works at the atomic level. By combining two atoms of hydrogen with one atom of oxygen, you get a new molecule—water—that has a whole new set of chemical properties. The same is true of all molecules. They have characteristic properties that differ from the properties of their constituent elements.

Compounds—A compound is a substance formed by the chemical combination of two or more elements. A compound has properties that are different from its constituent elements. Salt is a compound made of sodium and chlorine.

Mixtures—Most chemical reactions between elements create compounds, but it isn't always the case. Sometimes you mix two elements together, and while the molecules swirl around each other, no chemical change takes place, and the substances can be easily separated again. This is called a mixture, and the best analogy is the chocolate chip cookie. If you pretend cookie dough is one element and chocolate chips are another, you end up with a delicious Mixture Cookie. Think about it: you can pluck out each chip as you get to it, and it hasn't changed in taste or texture since when it was alone. The same goes for the cookie dough.

Energy

Energy is the capacity to do work or be active. Energy comes in many different forms. For example, a baseball resting on a high shelf has **potential energy**, which is energy derived from position rather than motion; it is energy that is stored until the object is released. In this case, if the baseball rolled off the shelf, it would convert its potential energy into **kinetic energy**—the energy of a moving object—as it plummeted towards the floor. If you picked up the baseball and placed it back on the shelf, you would be using up kinetic energy but the baseball would be gaining potential energy. When this happens, you should note that one form of energy is being replaced with another. This has to do with an important concept, the **conservation of energy principle**, which states:

•••••

Energy cannot be created or destroyed. Energy can be converted from one form to another, but the total quantity of energy in a system remains the same.

•••••

*T*he conservation of energy principle is also referred to as the **conservation of mass and energy**—because if mass is converted into energy, the quantity of mass and energy in the system remains the same.

That's why you have to keep putting gas in your car (which the car engine converts into energy that turns the wheels), food in your mouth (which your stomach breaks down into chemical compounds that the body's cells converts into fuel), and wood on a fire (if you want to remain warm, that is).

Basic Forms of Energy

Energy Type	Example
Solar	Sunlight
Electrical	Lightning
Chemical	A fire; the reaction of chemicals within a battery that produces an electric current

Motion

All physical objects have a certain **mass**, which is the amount of matter the object has. A sofa has more mass than a feather, for example. If a sofa is not moving, you need to exert force in order to move it. A **force** is an influence that changes the state of rest or motion of a body. Pushing or pulling on an object can change the motion of the object. Forces acting in the same direction (push) reinforce each other, while forces acting in different directions (pull) may cancel each other out. As you might imagine, the greater the mass of an object, the more force is required to move it (or stop it, if it is in motion). This is why pushing a sofa across a room is harder than pushing a feather across the same room.

Life Sciences

While physical science concerns itself with the Small Picture (atoms and such), much of life sciences is about the Big Picture. Items like food chains, Earth's ecosystems, and the cycle of water on earth are key topics in this branch of science.

The Food Chain

To begin with, a brief discussion of an ecosystem is in order. An **ecosystem** is formed by the interaction of a community of organisms with its environment (including nonliving things). Different types of ecosystems include the ocean, forest, desert, wetlands, and tundra. Organisms within an ecosystem always change the environment in which they live. When the environment changes, some of the plants and animals will survive, some will die, and others will relocate.

A **food chain** is the path that nutrients take in an ecosystem, where each member of the sequence of organisms feeds on the member below it. There are different food chains depending on climate, which is just the obvious way of saying animals in a desert do not eat or live the same way as animals in a rainforest. Here are two basic facts that relate to most food chains:

1) Most food chains begin with plants using sunlight, water, and mineral from the soil to grow.

2) All food chains end in the same place that they started.

Think of the life cycle of a little flower. It started off as a plant in a field, which grew using **chlorophyll**—the substance that makes plant leaves green—to combine sunlight, water, and minerals in the soil into energy. This plant was then eaten by a rabbit, which broke down the cellulose of the plant to use as energy for its own growth. A fox then came along, and since foxes eat meat, the rabbit provided the fox with a meal. Eventually, this fox dies, and its body ends up in a field. The minerals in the fox's body decompose and enter the soil. Through **photosynthesis**, a little flower takes these minerals and combines them with water and sunlight to create the energy it uses to grow, and everything starts over again.

Most food chains follow the pattern: plant ➜ herbivore (plant-eater) ➜ small carnivore (meat-eater) ➜ larger carnivore ➜ large carnivore dies, providing minerals for plants. Throughout the whole

Another large cycle is the cycle of water on earth, in which water rains down from a cloud, entering a brook. The brook feeds into a river, which empties out into an ocean. Sunlight—as you can see, sunlight plays a big role with life on this planet—evaporates the water, turning it into clouds which then travel over land. The water in the cloud condenses to form rain, which falls on the earth and enters a brook, starting the process over again.

process, matter is never destroyed, it just changes forms (similar to the conservation of mass and energy principle on page 117). Sunlight was used by the plant, plant matter was used by the rabbit, and rabbit meat was used by the fox. Overall, if you were to measure the quantity of matter (and energy) in the system, you would find it unchanged.

Cells

Cells are the basic unit of life, the smallest part of an organism that is capable of reproducing itself. All living creatures are composed of different kinds of cells. We humans have skin cells, heart cells, blood cells, and brain cells (to name a few), while plants have root cells, leaf cells, and other cells.

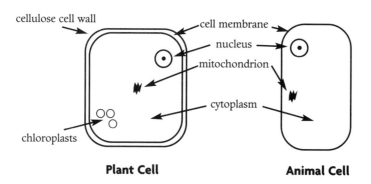

Plant Cell   **Animal Cell**

In grades three to five, your child will spend a lot of time learning about the similarities and differences between plants and animals in terms of structure, growth, and reproduction. Following is a rundown of some of the basic properties of both plant and animal cells.

Chloroplast—Found in plant cells, these structures contain chloro-

*S*ome organisms only have a single cell. *Protozoans* are any of a large group of single-celled microscopic organisms, including everybody's favorite single-celled organism, the amoeba. *Bacteria* are also single-celled, or unicellular, organisms.

phyll. The presence of chlorophyll is necessary for photosynthesis—the conversion of sunlight into energy—to occur (see page 119).

Cytoplasm—Everything in a cell outside the nucleus, but sometimes the word is used to refer to the jelly-like substance that all the organelles float around in.

Membrane—This is a thin layer that encloses a cell. This layer is usually **permeable**, which means that matter can pass through it. In a human cell, the membrane allows water and sugars to pass through.

Plant cell membranes are made out of a substance called **cellulose**. This differs from animal cell membranes, which are composed of fat and protein molecules.

Mitochondrion—This tiny structure found in the cytoplasm functions as cell's "power station," changing food to energy.

Nucleus—The cell nucleus is the tiny round body that controls the cell's activities. Most important, the nucleus contains **chromosomes**, tiny chromosomes comprised mostly of proteins and deoxyribonucleic acid, commonly referred to as DNA. DNA holds the genetic information of the cell.

There are other cell structures, but your child is unlikely to encounter them until later grades. Understanding the functions of the cell parts should be sufficient for most biology homework tasks.

Earth Science

A more precise name for this branch of study would be "Questions About What Makes Up the Earth." That would take too long to say, so science teachers stick with smaller titles like Geology and Weather, both of which fall under the banner *Earth Science*.

Geology

Basic geology questions ask about the composition of the earth, such as, "What is the center of the earth made of?" Snack enthusiasts might answer, "A rich, creamy filling," but sadly, the correct answer is "a large ball of semi-molten metal." In this sense, you can envision the earth as a monstrous dirt-covered piece of candy, but even if you had jaws big enough to bite into it, you shouldn't, since the center contains a very nasty surprise. Here is a cross-section diagram of the earth.

Cross Section of Earth

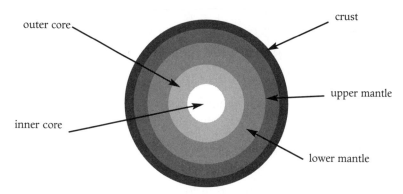

Following are some of the fundamental terms your child will encounter when studying geology:

Composition of the Earth
There are three major layers of the earth:

Crust—The outermost solid layer of the earth. There are two types of crust, oceanic and continental. The oceanic crust resides under the ocean, and is about six miles thick. The continental crust (what we stand on) is between twenty-five and forty-five miles in width.

Mantle—The layer of rock between the crust and the core. The mantle comprises about eighty percent of the earth's volume, and is over two thousand miles thick.

Core—The central portion of the earth (below the mantle) is made up primarily of an iron-nickel alloy. The outer core is liquid, while the inner core is solid, and the temperature of the core is estimated at over 7,000 degrees Fahrenheit. (However, no one has ever gone down to the core and actually proved that there's no rich creamy filling, so snack lovers still have reason to hope.)

Tectonic Plates

While your child is probably familiar with the idea of continents, a key distinction in geology is to think about tectonic plates. Tectonic plates are large portions of rigid rock just below the earth's surface. The continents and some of the ocean's floor rest on tectonic plates. Heat flow and movement of material within the earth makes these plates move. Not very fast, mind you: you won't have a tectonic plate sneak up on you while you are taking a nap in the park. However, tectonic plates are all in motion, and since the outermost level of the earth (that's the part we live on) is composed entirely of tectonic plates, this movement causes:

Earthquakes—A shaking or movement of the earth's surface, caused by the sudden shifting or rubbing together of tectonic plates. The place where the plates are rubbing is known as a **fault line.** The fault line in Southern California is one example.

Mountains—A raised portion of the earth's surface that's formed when two tectonic plates collide below the surface and one pushes the other one up.

Valleys—When two tectonic plates are moving apart, they cause depressions in the earth's surface, and valleys like the Great Rift Valley are created.

Volcanoes—An opening in the surface of the earth from which melted rock and gases flow; the material that flows out often builds up around the hole to form a mountain.

While earthquakes and volcanoes can change the Earth's surface rapidly, other events work slowly, yet cause great changes just the same. For example, **erosion** is the gradual wearing away of rock or dirt by the actions of waves or wind. The Appalachian Mountains in the eastern United States were much taller millennia ago, but the constant removal of dirt by the wind has caused them to lose a great deal of height. In a similar manner, coastlines are often shifting back and forth due to the erosion caused by the pounding of waves along the shore.

Rock Types

When you think about geology, you have to think about rocks. There are three main types:

Igneous—Rocks formed from very hot liquid matter, such as magma, that has cooled and solidified. Granite is one example.

Metamorphic—Formed when high pressure and heat meet with a sedimentary or igneous rock, resulting in a change in composition. Marble is formed by the metamorphic effects of heat and pressure on limestone.

Sedimentary—Rocks formed by the compression of particles that have settled at the bottom of rivers, lakes, and oceans. Limestone is a good example: it's formed from the compression of the remains of sea creatures.

Weather

Energy from the sun heats the earth unevenly, which causes the air to move around and create weather patterns. Questions about the weather can revolve around subjects like:

Clouds—Clouds are masses of condensed water vapor. If they are low-lying, they are called fog or mist. Your child may be asked to learn to recognize types of clouds (such as cirrus, cumulus, stratus, and thunderheads) by their shapes, their height from the ground, and the kind of precipitation they contain.

Precipitation—Water that falls from the air as rain, sleet, snow, and hail.

Temperature—When talking about weather, temperature refers to the degree of hotness or coldness of the air. Air temperature has a big impact on the movement of **air masses,** which are large bodies of air with only small variations in temperatures and levels of humidity, or moisture. The meeting of air masses of different characteristics causes much of our weather.

Wind patterns—To understand wind, think back to the definition of a gas. The atmosphere is composed of particles, and if you have more particles in one area than another, you have a high-pressure area (the greater number of molecules creates pressure). Like people moving from a crowded apartment to an empty house, particles like to go where they have some elbow-room. When air particles travel from a high-pressure area to a low-pressure area, you get wind.

When studying geology and the weather, your child is likely to encounter "what if" questions that require her to show that she understands the relationships between the forces and cycles of the earth. For example:

EXAMPLE:

Give one example each of how human activities change Earth's land, oceans, and atmosphere.

If your child presents you with a question like this, your first step should be to figure out the type of answer the teacher wants, and you can do this by looking through your child's notebook or textbook. For example, your child's teacher may have been talking about the environmental impact of things like deforestation (the cutting down of large numbers of trees), farming, irrigation, sewage, and carbon monoxide emission from cars. Once you see the kinds of terms she has been working with, help your child think of examples. Ask her questions like:

- What are some of the things humans do to the land?

- Can the resources humans use to make these products be replaced?

- What products do humans make that go into the atmosphere?

- What human products go into the ocean?

Once she answers these questions, help her think of some of the ways these actions and products affect the environment.

Space Sciences

In grade school, your child's study of Space Sciences will involve learning the basics about the planets and the solar system. Here is a quick crib sheet on the solar system.

A solar system consists of a star and all the objects—planets, comets, asteroids—that revolve around it. Our solar system resides in a galaxy known as the Milky Way, which contains at least 100 billion other stars.

Asteroids—An asteroid is sometimes called a minor planet becasue asteroids and planets are very similar. Asteroids are composed of rock and iron and orbit the sun: the main difference between asteroids and planets is one of size. Most asteroids in our solar system lie in an asteroid belt located between Mars and Jupiter.

Comets—Imagine a million-foot-tall person throwing a dirty snowball from outside our solar system. A comet is like that snowball.

Composed usually of water and ice, comets travel on highly curved paths through the solar system. Sometimes they pass close enough that they can be seen in the sky. As the comets travel through the solar system, they lose bits of dust and rock. These pieces, called **meteoroids**, fall to Earth at great speeds and burn up in the atmosphere. A large number of these pieces falling at the same time is known as a meteor shower.

Earth—The third planet from the sun, about seventy percent of Earth's surface is composed of water. As far as we know, our planet is the only one that sustains life.

Moon—Our moon is a large chunk of rock that circles Earth. It is kept in this orbit by Earth's gravitational field. Other planets have moons, too; some even have several moons.

Planets—A planet is a large celestial object in orbit around a star. A planet can be made of rocks and metals, like Earth, or it can be composed primarily of gas (like Jupiter). The nine planets in our solar system are: Mercury, Venus, Earth, Mars, Jupiter, Saturn, Uranus, Neptune, and Pluto. The planets are listed in order of how close they are to the sun.

Sun—That big yellow ball in the sky that we call the sun is a star. The sun, a typical star, is a huge ball of gas that produces vast amounts of energy as a result of nuclear reactions taking place inside it. These reactions are so powerful that their energy (in the form of sunlight) reaches our planet even though Earth is millions of miles away.

The sun is the biggest thing in this solar system, and Earth and all the other planets are caught in its **gravitational pull** (the force of attraction between two bodies). This causes the planets to rotate around the sun.

Explaining the Solar System

Before explaining the solar system, you should gather together a table lamp, an orange, and a golf ball, or objects that are similar to these. A problem your child, and many people, may have with astronomy is that the topics being explained are just so large. Envisioning the earth, sun, moon, and all the other planets spinning around in huge cosmic orbits can cause a headache. This brings about a famous bit of advice:

When discussing astronomy, always keep a good supply of spherically-shaped fruit around. When the homework is over, eat the planets.

Earth Orbiting the Sun

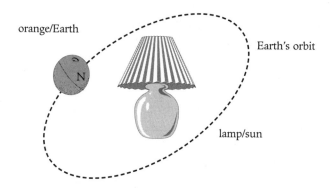

The earth (orange) travels around the sun (lamp) in an ellipse, which is like a flattened circle. The earth is tilted, so draw a horizontal line around the middle of the orange to represent the equator and then shift it at a slight angle.

Once you do this, you see that more sunlight is falling on the northern half of the orange than the southern half. This causes summer in the northern part of the earth and winter in the southern part. If you move the orange around 180 degrees, you get the opposite situation. This leads to summer in the southern part of the world and winter in the northern part.

At the **equator**, the imaginary line around the middle of the earth (halfway between the North and South Poles), it's pretty much hot all the time.

While the orange is travelling in its big circuit around the sun, it is also spinning. This spinning cuases various parts of the orange to rotate in and out of the sunlight. These light and dark cycles last about twenty-four hours and are what we call *days*.

Long-Term Science Projects and the Scientific Method

Many long-term science projects involve setting up an experiment and drawing conclusions from the results.

Suppose your child came up to you after dinner and proclaimed, "I want to be the greatest mad scientist the world has ever known." Rather than reminding him that mad scientists only exist in old black-and-white movies, you should praise him for his lofty goals and then send him off to study the Scientific Method (also known as scientific inquiry).

Note: While your third-grade child probably won't be assigned a science experiment to conduct at home, the procedures detailed in the scientific method are the basis for the type of work he is doing now, such as differentiating evidence from opinion or predicting the result of an experiment and comparing it with the outcome.

The Scientific Method

1. Pose a question.

This is similar to coming up with a good main idea for an English essay. Consider a life sciences experiment in which your child will test various fertilizers to see which one works best with bean plants. The question in this scientific experiment would be, "Which of these three fertilizers—eggshells, cough medicine, or plastic action figurines—works best to help bean plants grow?" Your child would then set up a scientific experiment to try and answer this question.

2. Suggest a plausible answer/Develop a hypothesis.

A **hypothesis** is an educated guess that can be tested. So to develop a hypothesis for the fertilizer experiment, you could say, "The cough medicine will help the plants the most; since it makes people feel better, it should make bean plants feel better." This might not be the best guess, but it isn't crucial to have the correct hypothesis every time. The results of your experiment will either confirm or deny your hypothesis, so you can always revise your hypothesis in light of any new evidence uncovered.

3. Test the idea by conducting an experiment.

This is the key aspect of the scientific method. Your child must set up his experiment so that only the main question is being tested.

To do this in the bean plant fertilizer experiment, brainstorm with your child about all the different variables that could affect plant growth. You might come up with a list that contains many of these variables:

1) Amount of sunlight received

2) Amount of water received

3) Type of soil

4) Amount of soil in pot

5) Amount of exposure plant has to Tibbles, the plant-eating cat

6) Type of fertilizer used

These six variables all affect bean plant growth, but your child's experiment is interested only in number 6, the type of fertilizer. Therefore, to make this a proper scientific experiment, you must ensure that the other five factors are equal among the test plants in order for the results to have any meaning.

This means each test plant receives the exact same amount of sunlight and water, is planted in the same type of soil, has the same amount of soil, and is protected from Tibbles equally. With these five factors all equal, the remaining factor is "type of fertilizer." Therefore, any difference in plant growth between the test plants can be attributed to the different fertilizers used.

The correct set-up for this experiment would consist of four plants in identical pots, with identical soil, given similar amounts of sunlight and water. Plant 1 would receive 4 grams of egg shells each day (placed in the soil), Plant 2 would get 4 grams of cough medicine, while Plant 3 would receive 4 grams of plastic action figure placed in its soil. The results of each plant's growth would be measured each day—at the same time every day—for a period of two weeks.

You may have noticed that there are four plants total, but only Plants 1-3 receive fertilizer. Plant 4 illustrates the idea of a **control group**. A control group is a group in an experiment that is not manipulated. In this experiment, no fertilizer is given to the control group plant so that your child can discover how a plant would grow without the effect of any fertilizer. In this experiment, a control group is important because it helps your child determine whether any of the fertilizers actually aid growth.

4. Record results and determine whether hypothesis is correct.

After two weeks, your child will have collected data on the growth of four bean plants. Let's suppose his final results were the following:

Plant	Final Height
Plant 1 (eggshells)	10 inches
Plant 2 (cough medicine)	2 inches
Plant 3 (plastic)	7 inches
Plant 4 (Control)	7 inches

With these results, you can see that the original hypothesis was not correct: cough medicine was not the best fertilizer (egg shells were). Having a control group plant lets your child make further statements, however. Since you know that a bean plant with no fertilizer would have grown seven inches, and the cough medicine plant only grew two inches, you can state that, "Our experiment showed that cough medicine was harmful to bean plant growth." If you did not have a control group, there would be no way to make this statement. In grade school, when the result of the experiment doesn't confirm the hypothesis, your child will be encouraged to reformulate ideas based on the evidence, as well as analyze alternative explanations and procedures.

Reporting the Results of an Experiment

At this point, your child will have completed a successful experiment using the scientific method. This might be sufficient in itself, but in the later grades she will probably be asked to publish the results of her experiment. This would include a brief report about the structure of the experiment and the results, as well as a chart or graph representing the results.

Writing the Report

Your child's report can be brief and can follow the structure of the scientific method itself. The first paragraph would describe the question being addressed; the second paragraph would describe the hypothesis; the third paragraph would describe the experimental design; and the fourth paragraph would describe the results of the experiment and any possible new approaches to answering the original question.

Representing Data

A simple chart or graph is usually all that is needed to represent the result of an experiment. For example, we might represent the results of our plant experiment using a line graph showing the growth rate of our plants over two weeks.

A Review of Basic Social Studies Concepts for Grades 3-5

GRADE SCHOOL SOCIAL STUDIES FOCUSES on Geography, Economics, Civics, and History. These are all large topics, and we can't summarize them completely in this chapter. Instead, we will give you a quick refresher and a framework for approaching these topics, examples of the kinds of homework questions your child might encounter, and tips for addressing those questions.

Geography

Maps and General Map Skills

Maps provide a much-needed visual component to historical events, which is why geography is so important. While a globe will show the actual distance Columbus traveled, other maps can provide

Encouraging your child to watch or read the news daily will help him with his social studies work. Many current events are covered in social studies class, since a current political situation can often be explained in light of past events.

students with a wealth of information about land and the people on it. To help your child with his social studies, then, there are two main duties you should try to fulfill.

1. Provide him with access to maps.

If your child has a computer in his study area, then a CD-ROM atlas is an excellent purchase. Whatever area of the world your child is studying, he can punch it up on the computer screen to view it. This will help him understand events more clearly, as it is much easier for him to visualize the difficulties the American troops faced during the American Revolution if he has a map of the area in front of him.

If your child doesn't have access to a computer, that is not a problem. However, your child should have a good atlas or some form of fold-out world map or globe that he can refer to if necessary. Some maps are quite nice, and make great posters for a study area. Even if your child starts avoiding homework by staring at the map, at least he will be learning geography at some level.

If you get a CD-ROM atlas, it is a good idea to get one that provides a variety of information besides just political boundaries. Some CD-ROMs will have maps showing population densities, educational levels, birth rates, and other data. This will help your child learn more about a country.

2. Help your child analyze the information on a map.

Many maps come chock full of information: political boundaries, rivers, mountain ranges, major roads, deserts, swamps, airports, electrical substations, national parks, intermittent salt lakes, and capitals are all marked in an area the size of your hand. While in third grade your child's geography instruction will deal primarily with local land features, such as the local lake, mountain, or highway, in fourth and fifth grades your child will learn about the world's geography: the continents, oceans, major mountain ranges, and more.

If your child's homework requires him to interpret this information and he's having difficulty, then the first place to look is the map's key. Every map and globe has a **key** that explains how everything is ordered.

The key often contains symbols, and these symbols vary from map to map. If you and your child take it one question at a time, map questions should not be overwhelming. If the question talks about how many miles it is from Point Q to City R, you will need to use the **map scale**, which shows how many miles equals one inch on the map. Then it is just a matter of getting your child to use the ruler he keeps in his homework area to measure the distance in inches and then convert it to miles.

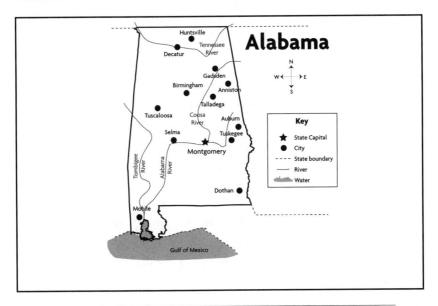

EXAMPLE:

On the map provided, draw a circle around the capital of
Alabama and make a list of all rivers shown.

This is a question about map reading. As mentioned before, the first step is to check the key, which reveals that the state capital is marked with a star. Your child just needs to search for and circle the star to answer this part of the question correctly. The key also reveals that rivers are marked by dotted lines. Your child now needs to look for the dotted lines and the names written over them and make a list of all the names he sees.

Economics

A basic understanding of economic concepts is very helpful to your child's understanding of the society in which she lives.

Supply and Demand

Supply and demand determine the price of an object. **Supply** means how many of a particular good or service are available for purchase. **Demand** refers to how many people wish to purchase a particular good or service. Let us use silkworms and roaches as an example. Suppose your child wanted to go into business selling these two insects as pets. She discovers that many people like the idea of making their own silk (although technically the worm's going to do all the work), so the demand for silkworms is high. In fact, the demand is much greater than the supply of silkworms, and your child realizes that she can charge twice as much for each silkworm and still find takers.

Therefore, since demand exceeds supply, the price of an item increases. On the other

The United States—and most of the world, for that matter—now use money as a means of currency, so prices will refer to dollars and cents. However, it was not always this way. Early human civilizations used barter, the exchange of one item for another, instead of money, so one pig might be worth five jars of olive oil. Even so, the law of supply and demand still operated, since an increase in demand for pigs would lead to a change in the exchange rate: say, one pig might now get you eight jars of olive oil.

side, no one is interested in buying cockroaches. And unfortunately, there are a lot of cockroaches. Since the supply of cockroaches exceeds demand, the price of cockroaches will fall, probably all the way down to 100 cockroaches for $ 0.01.

EXAMPLE:

Maya Root Coffeehouse has been in business in Centerville for 20 years serving a small selection of imported coffee drinks for $3 a cup. It has enjoyed a limited, but devoted, clientele. Last month, a new Ishmael Coffee Stand shop—one of a national chain of over 500 Ishmael Coffee Stands—opened down the block offering a wide variety of imported coffee drinks for $2 a cup. What economic impact might this have on Maya Root?

This is the kind of question your child's teacher might give her to test whether she understands supply and demand. While no one can completely predict public behavior, certain assumptions can be made about the situation described above. There is no perfectly right answer to this question, but as long as your child can use economic principles to support herself, she should be fine.

When your child is having trouble answering a question like this, you can help her by asking leading questions. Using the example above, some appropriate leading questions might be:

- Why do you think Maya Root's clientele was so small to begin with?

- If Maya Root's clientele was so small, why do you think it stayed in business?

- Do you think the prices offered by Ishmael's will make a difference in the number of customers it attracts?

- What kinds of things can Maya Root do to become competitive?

These types of questions will help your child pick out the important elements provided in the question, and then expand upon them to develop a response.

Production and Consumption

Something that is made is **produced**, while something used or ingested is **consumed**. Production is often used on a large scale, to say something like, "Production of tiny cars has vastly exceeded consumers' current needs." This is just another way of saying that tiny car makers made a lot of tiny cars that no one wanted to buy.

Goods and Services

In general, all jobs can be placed into one of these categories. **Goods** are anything that's created that someone wants or needs; doughnuts, tires, squeaky shoes, and paintings of dogs playing poker are all examples of goods produced. A **service** is the performance of work for someone else. For example, providing financial advice, medical care, and tutoring sessions are all services.

Civics

At the grade school level, civics covers a wide territory, from learning that actions have consequences to the importance of local and national symbols, landmarks, and documents. In this section, we will discuss the ideal model for how the American government is supposed to work, although sometimes your child's classroom discussions will revolve around whether the government *actually* works that way.

In America, we consider the ideal model of government to be a **democracy**, a system of government in which the people hold ultimate power and select their government representatives (the people who run the government) in free elections. In grade school your child will learn about the influence of the Declaration of Independence and the Constitution on our democracy.

The Declaration of Independence

This document is important because it announced the creation of a separate, new nation known as the United States. It was written chiefly by Thomas Jefferson in 1776, which was at the beginning of the American Revolution against England.

The Declaration states that all men are created equal, and that everyone has the right to life, liberty, and the pursuit of happiness.

The United States Constitution

The Articles of the Constitution established the United States government and its system of laws, and it is the system of government that we still use today. The Constitution defines the rights to which all Americans are entitled and describes the three main branches of government:

Executive Branch—This branch includes the President and Vice President of the United States, but it also includes all Cabinet members and agencies, which are appointed by the President. The function of the executive branch is to carry out laws passed by the legislative branch.

Legislative Branch—This is the United States Congress, which is a **bicameral** body since it is composed of two separate houses, the Senate and the House of Representatives. The function of Congress is to make laws.

Judicial Branch—This includes the Supreme Court, the highest court in the country, as well as the other courts throughout the country. The function of

Your child might also be introduced to the concept of **checks and balances**, a division of the powers of the different branches of our government that is designed to insure that no one branch of the government can become too strong and overpower the others. A good analogy to this is the rock/scissors/paper game you play with your hand if you need to decide who has to get up and bring in more snacks when your family is watching a movie. In the game, rock beats scissors, but loses to paper. Each item is strong in some way, but can be defeated by another item. The system of checks and balances requires the three branches of government to work together.

the judicial branch is to explain and apply the laws passed by the legislative branch.

Federal and State Powers

Our government is founded on a belief in **federalism**, which is a system of government wherein power is shared between national and state governments. Both the national and state governments have exclusive powers (meaning that the other one doesn't have that power), such as the power of the federal government to regulate interstate trade and declare war, or the power of the state governments to issue certain licenses and regulate intrastate trade. The national and state governments also share powers, such as the power to collect taxes, build roads, and enforce laws. So while our government today places most of its power in the hands of Congress, the President, and the Supreme Court, their powers can be checked by those of the states, and vice versa.

Learning about civics requires good, old-fashioned memorization along with the ability to draw some conclusions about the way our government works. Here is an example of the type of homework question your child might see:

EXAMPLE:

Who were the main framers of the Constitution and what roles did they play in drafting and ratifying the document?

This is a straight factual question that requires little independent thought. The goal is to get your child to memorize the names and actions of our founding fathers. The information your child needs to answer this question will probably be in her notes or textbook. If not, a quick search in the encyclopedia will reveal the answer.

History

*H*istory homework, like most homework, comes in two general types: fact-based questions and complicated questions that require the formation of theories and the drawing of conclusions.

Fact-Based Questions

If your child comes to you with a very specific historical question, such as, "When was the Treaty of Ghent signed?" there's no use trying to bluff that you know the answer. Your child has heard all the good excuses—in fact, creating new and better excuses takes up an enormous part of his average day—and your old ones will not fool him.

You duty is to help your child find the exact answer, and this means looking in the following places, in this order:

1. The textbook

If your child did not look for the answer here already, you may chide him gently for it. He should be aware of whether or not his teacher gave the class questions that could be found in the reading, or if the teacher told them they would have to do some research. If your child did look but just did not locate it, that's okay; if it becomes a regular occurrence, though, this may reveal that your child is not absorbing much of what he is reading. If this is the case, you may want to make sure his reading skills are up to par.

2. A general reference book or encyclopedia CD-ROM

If your child has a book or CD-ROM nearby, you should have him search on his own at first before joining in. If your child doesn't find the answer on his own, look in a general history book with a good index. Go to the index, look up Treaty of Ghent, and see if you can find an answer there. A CD-ROM word search should get you the answer as well.

3. The Internet

If you have a computer, go to a search engine, type in Treaty of

Ghent, and see what links pop up. It is a good idea to stick to sites that end in *.edu,* since these are educational sites, such as colleges.

4. The library

The answer will be there, but keep in mind that homework need not be perfect every time. If your child has a lot of unanswered historical questions, a trip might be warranted. However, don't spend a huge chunk of time tracking down a single fact, unless your child has developed a quest-like fervor for the answer. Spending an entire evening searching for one answer is not an efficient use of time, especially if it breeds rancor in your child and exhaustion in you.

Essay Questions

Complicated history questions are much like complicated English questions. They ask your child to approach an historical topic for a certain point of view or to compare certain historical events. The same principles for addressing English literature questions apply here. See the "Six Questions" sidebar on page 103 for help.

Long-Term Social Studies Projects

*L*ong-term social studies projects are usually two- to five-page research papers focused on history. They require research, writing, and grammar skills, so the approach discussed on pages 105–112 will work well here.

Your child may also be asked to draw on different types of research materials to complete a project. These materials are usually broken down into two categories:

Primary Sources

Primary sources are things like historical documents, interviews, letters, and diaries. These are actual historical artifacts that may or may not have been interpreted or explained by a critic or scholar before.

Secondary Sources

These are things like scholarly books and articles. Secondary sources offer explanations and interpretations of events and materials and usually rely on primary sources for back-up. Authors of secondary source material may also rely on other secondary sources.

Using secondary source material is a skill your child will focus on in grades three to five. Every time she looks up something in a encyclopedia, she is using a secondary source. Using primary sources is trickier and more advanced: it will proably not be broached until the fifth grade, if then. When it does appear, it may take the form of an interview. Your child will be asked to question someone about their job, and then discuss what she learned in class.

Fencing Lessons
and A Final Word

MANY STUDENTS WILL NEED HELP on topics that fall outside of the major areas covered in this book. If your child is taking fencing lessons, for example, we really have not given you any pointers to pass on to him. Okay, here's one—keep your elbow extended when lunging—but that's it. Our fencing days are over.

If your child's homework assignment consists of learning to play the scales on his French horn, don't worry that you have never picked up the instrument in your life. In this case, and in others, you won't be able to impart the correct knowledge to him at a moment's notice. But regardless of the subject matter, when your child asks you for help on his homework you can always be supportive, caring, and kind when answering. If you don't know the answer, and the two of you search and can't find the answer, don't get frustrated and upset. Keep in mind there's a larger issue at stake, which is the relationship between you and your child.

Mutual caring and respect between the two of you will always be more important than any one fact, so if you find yourself losing your composure because you and your child cannot find out what year the Treaty of Ghent was signed, don't get upset. Reassure your child that homework doesn't have to be perfect every time, and he can always learn from his mistakes. This positive, caring attitude—more than any one fact—is what will make you a Homework Hero in the eyes of your child.

By the way, the Treaty of Ghent was signed in 1814.

Homework on the World Wide Web

If you have a computer with an Internet connection, you might like to take a peek at these homework-related sites:

Bigchalk.com
http://www.bigchalk.com

B.J. Pinchbeck's Homework Helper
http://school.discovery.com/homeworkhelp/bjpinchbeck/index.html

Dictionary.com
http://www.dictionary.com

DiscoverySchool.com
http://school.discovery.com/students/

Fact Monster.com
http://www.factmonster.com/homework/

Homeworkspot.com
http://www.homeworkspot.com/

Thesaurus.com
http://www.thesaurus.com/

Yahooligans! School Bell: Homework Help
http://www.yahooligans.com/school_bell/homework_help/

Information for parents of children with learning differences
http://www.SchwabLearning.com

Other Books by Priscilla L. Vail, M.A.T.

A Language Yardstick: Understanding and Assessment
About Dyslexia: Unraveling the Myth
Clear and Lively Writing: Language Games and Activities for Everyone
Common Ground: Phonics and Whole Language Working Together
Emotion: The On/Off Switch for Learning
Gifted, Precocious, or Just Plain Smart
Learning Styles: Food for Thought and 130 Practical Tips
Reading Comprehension: Students' Needs and Teachers' Tools
Smart Kids with School Problems: Things to Know and Ways to Help
Third and Fourth Grade Language Assessment
*Words Fail Me!: How Language Works and What Happens When It
    Doesn't*
The World of the Gifted Child

Acknowledgements

Drew and Cynthia Johnson would like to thank their friends—Frank, Jeff, Renee, John, Sam, and Kelly—at Magnolia Café South and Vulcan Video South for keeping them well-fed and visually entertained during the course of writing this book.